NATIONAL WILDLIFE FEDERATION®

ATTRACTING

Birds, Butterflies
and Other Backyard Wildlife

DAVID MIZEJEWSKI

CREATIVE
HOMEOWNER®

CRE🏠TIVE
HOMEOWNER®

Creative Homeowner® is a registered trademark of New Design Originals Corporation.

Senior Editor: Fran J. Donegan
Copy Editor: Ellen Ellender
Assistant Editor: Jennifer Ramcke
Indexer: Schroeder Indexing Services
Senior Designer: Glee Barre
Cover Design: David Geer
Illustrations: Michele Farrar
Illustration Sources: (page 76) Bat Conservation International; (page 85) Northern Prairie Wildlife Research Center and North American Bluebird Society
Cover Photography: (main image) Daybreak Imagery; (insets) *top and middle* Daybreak Imagery; *bottom* Gerry Bishop
Back Cover Photography: *top* Daybreak Imagery; *left* Connie Toops; *right* Daybreak Imagery; *author's photograph* Mary T. Crimmings

Current Printing (last digit)
20 19 18 17 16 15 14

Manufactured in China

Attracting Birds, Butterflies, and Other Backyard Wildlife
Library of Congress Control Number: 2003112917
ISBN: 1-58011-150-5

CREATIVE HOMEOWNER®
www.creativehomeowner.com

Creative Homeowner books are distributed exclusively by
Fox Chapel Publishing
1970 Broad Street
East Petersburg, PA 17520
www.FoxChapelPublishing.com

DEDICATION

To Mom and Dad:

All those years of muddy clothes, poison ivy, and

the zoo in my bedroom paid off. Thanks for allowing

me to pursue my passion for nature.

Certify Your Wildlife-Friendly Yard!

Add your new wildlife-friendly yard to the national registry of official Wildlife Habitat™ sites. Benefits of certification include:

- A personalized certificate suitable for framing
- A quarterly e-newsletter full of gardening tips
- NWF membership, which includes a subscription to *National Wildlife* magazine
- Recognition for your hard work

Visit www.nwf.org/certify for more information!

Follow these four simple steps (and see pages 120–121)

1. **Grow native plants** found in your area, including trees, shrubs, and other plants that offer food such as pollen, nectar, nuts, cones, berries, and other seeds.

2. **Provide water for wildlife** with a small pond, birdbath, or shallow dish ... or care for a natural spring or stream on or near your habitat.

3. **Create protective cover** for wildlife by growing a meadow, a prairie, densely branched shrubs, and when appropriate, evergreens. Place hollow logs and rock piles in your yard.

4. **Build birdhouses;** attach to metal poles; and monitor their use. Grow host plants for butterfly and moth caterpillars to eat, and provide dense plantings to create safe areas for nesting wildlife.

TABLE OF CONTENTS

Introduction

As we enter the 21st century, natural places and the wildlife species that inhabit them face ever increasing pressure from human activity. Today, there are few places on Earth that have not been affected by the way and the rate at which we build and maintain our homes, farms, and cities. As a result, natural habitat is disappearing at an alarming rate, and habitat loss is the number one threat to wildlife today.

Wildlife species and the natural areas they need to survive are important and should be protected and restored. Imagine life without the song of birds and the chirring of crickets, the beauty of a windswept prairie, or the cool serenity of a green woodland. Imagine a child growing up without having the opportunity to watch a tadpole changing into a frog, to smell a

▲ The right conditions will invite a host of birds, butterflies, and other species to your yard.

▶ Planting native plant species is the key to attracting wildlife.

▶ Bird feeders supplement plant food sources.

wildflower, or to wade in a clear stream. Without wild areas, humanity, as well as wildlife, suffers.

It is easy to feel as if there is no hope for wildlife in our modern world of asphalt, smog, and traffic. But there is hope. You can choose to create a garden or landscape that helps restore the ecological balance in your yard. You can surround yourself with beautiful native plants that will attract wildlife and allow you to observe an amazing array of wildlife every day.

This book will teach you how to restore wildlife habitat in your own yard or other garden space, and how to get it certified by the National Wildlife Federation® as an official Backyard Wildlife Habitat™ site. In doing so, you will be doing your part to restore the ecology of the land on which you live.

chapter one

Habitat Basics

The secret to attracting birds, butterflies, and other wonderful wildlife to your backyard lies in restoring their natural habitat. You'll take a giant step toward inviting wildlife into your yard by providing the conditions they need to survive and thrive. The National Wildlife Federation® has grouped these needs into four categories: food, water, cover, and places for wildlife to bear and raise their young.

◄ You will attract wildlife species to your yard by restoring their natural habitat.

VANISHING HABITATS

Many wildlife species are losing habitat at an unprecedented rate. Habitat loss sometimes occurs as a result of natural disasters, such as earthquakes, volcanic activity, flooding, or severe storms, but these happen so infrequently that wildlife populations soon recover. Unfortunately, human activity is the most significant cause of the destruction and degradation of quality habitat for wildlife today. As the human population grows, it competes with wildlife for resources and space. Mankind's agricultural and land development practices increasingly alter the landscape in ways that render it barren for wildlife.

But you can change some of these conditions by creating a wildlife habitat in your own yard and throughout your community. By planting native plants—plants that would grow in the area naturally— and taking a few other steps, you can restore the components of habitat and invite the wildlife back to the land it once occupied. The National Wildlife Federation's Backyard Wildlife

Habitat™ program has been helping people do this for over 30 years. More than 40,000 homeowners have restored the natural habitats in their yards. Today, these people host the birds, butterflies, and other wildlife that had once avoided their yards.

RESTORING HABITATS

Creating a wildlife habitat is more than just planting a pretty garden. It's actually restoring one small piece of the ecosystem. Before starting out to create a natural habitat, it is important to realize that all plant and animal species have an impact on and are affected by other living organisms and the environment around them. Science refers to this interaction as an ecosystem. Healthy ecosystems are balanced. If you understand this principle and apply it to your garden and landscape plans, you'll create a balanced, self-sustaining mini-ecosystem that supports birds, butterflies, and a wide variety of wildlife species.

▲ When planning your garden, look to natural ecosystems such as this woodland for inspiration.

◄ This prairie is one example of a self-sustaining ecosystem.

THE IMPORTANCE OF BALANCE

In any given region, the plants, animals, and other living organisms have interacted with one other and the environment around them for millions of years. As a result of this interaction, species adapt, stabilize, and change over time. The natural result is plant and animal species that have formed interacting communities—an ecosystem. Healthy ecosystems achieve balance when communities are diverse and self-sustaining.

UPSETTING THE BALANCE

Native plant and animal species occur naturally in a given region. When people move a plant or animal from its native habitat to a new one, the plant or animal becomes an exotic, or alien, species in the new area.

Don't confuse the introduction of an exotic species with the natural course of evolution. Species naturally move into new areas when resources become available to them. This natural process takes millions of years, exotic species are now being introduced at a rate that is hundreds or thousands of times faster than would occur naturally. Native species cannot adapt to the abrupt introduction of new species.

Some exotic plants or animals become invasive. They spread rampantly and compete with native species for space and resources because the predators or parasites that would naturally keep their population in check do not exist in the new area. Left unchecked, invasive plant species can change diverse, balanced

◀ A successful backyard habitat relies on the plant species that grow and thrive naturally in a given area.

native plant communities into monocultures—areas where only one species can grow—and can push other species to the point of extinction. Often, invasive species are those that reproduce quickly and can survive a variety of conditions.

▲ An invasive species, such as this English ivy (*Hedera helix*), can quickly spread and push out other types of plants.

◀ Wildlife naturally developed along with the available food sources. Here a gray catbird enjoys a shad-blow serviceberry (*Amelanchier canadensis*).

PROBLEMS CAUSED BY EXOTIC PLANTS

One problem with exotic plants is that they often look green, lush, and "natural" to most people. Many gardeners and wildlife watchers who have adopted organic gardening practices and fight to keep natural areas from development are unwittingly planting exotic, or invasive, species in their gardens.

One ornamental plant, Chinese wisteria (*Wisteria sinensis*), is an example of a species that is invasive in much of North America. While this species of wisteria has beautiful lavender blossoms with an amazing scent, it can do serious ecological damage to native plant and wildlife communities. When it escapes the garden and invades woodlands, it out-competes or simply smothers dozens of species of woodland wildflowers, ferns, sedges, shrubs, and small trees, each with a unique collection of wildlife species that depend upon them. Japanese wisteria (*Wisteria floribunda*) is also invasive.

Another example of an invasive exotic plant is purple loosestrife (*Lythrum salicaria*), a popular ornamental plant sold by nurseries across the country. It is native to Europe and grows in wet areas such as marshes, wet meadows, floodplains, and even roadside ditches. It has tall spikes of showy purple flowers that

▲ Purple loosestrife (*Lythrum salicaria*) is an ornamental plant that can be harmful to natural habitats.

▶ The berries to the right are from a native dogwood and a source of food to local birds; those to the far right are from an exotic dogwood and inedible.

last all summer long. Its only problem is that it has escaped human cultivation and invaded natural wetland areas. In places where purple loosestrife has invaded, naturally diverse and productive wetland ecosystems that once supported hundreds of species of different native wetland plants, waterfowl, insects, amphibians, and their predators have now become barren monocultures. Fortunately, the dangers posed to natural areas by this invasive exotic plant have begun to be recognized, and the plant is now listed on many noxious weed lists and even banned in some states. Despite this, it is still available for purchase in some nurseries. Many other invasives are still commonly available as well.

DISEASE CARRIERS

In addition to the threat of becoming invasive, exotic plants can also harbor diseases that can kill native species. The American chestnut (*Castanea dentate*) was once the dominant tree in the eastern half of North America. In 1904, an Asian chestnut disease was accidentally introduced to North America from exotic chestnuts planted in New York. American chestnuts had no natural defenses to this exotic blight, and it quickly became an epidemic. Today, there are no healthy mature chestnuts left in North America.

A more recent example is the introduction of an exotic anthracnose (a type of fungus) that slowly kills the native Pacific dogwood (*Cornus nuttallii*) of the West and the flowering dog-

▲ The Asian kousa dogwood (*Cornus Kousa*) is often used in place of native dogwood species.

17

habitat hints:
THE PROBLEMS WITH EXOTICS

- Exotics can become invasive and degrade naturally diverse ecosystems.
- Exotics can introduce and harbor diseases that afflict native species.
- Exotics do not support the same number of insects, which are the food source for many native wildlife species.
- Some exotics require maintenance and wasteful watering and chemicals.

wood (*Cornus florida*) of the East. Pacific and flowering dogwoods coevolved with the wildlife species that share their native ranges, and they produce berries at the same time that birds begin their autumn migration.

Some evidence suggests that the exotic dogwood anthracnose was introduced by the Asian kousa dogwood (*Cornus kousa*), which is often used as an ornamental landscape tree. Kousa dogwood is much less susceptible to the anthracnose and can host it without succumbing to it, unlike native dogwoods. Because the anthracnose rarely kills kousa dogwood, many tree-care professionals recommend planting it instead of Pacific or flowering dogwoods. Planting disease-resistant species makes sense from a conventional gardening perspective, but it doesn't take into account the needs of wildlife. Kousa dogwood produces fruits that are twice as large as native dogwood berries and inedible to most birds. (See page 17.) They might also be helping to spread the exotic anthracnose. Replacing native dogwoods with exotic ones is a bad ecological choice that could negatively affect migratory songbirds and other wildlife species.

EXOTICS AND PREY SPECIES

Another problem posed by the widespread use of exotics is that they often don't support prey species, without which many predatory wildlife can't survive. Many insects find exotics unpalatable, which is one reason they are used in our gardens. In areas where exotics have become invasive, the populations of insects can decline. Many wildlife species—birds in particular—depend on a steady source of insects to feed themselves and their young.

Additionally, unlike native plants, the

exotic plants that don't become invasive by surviving and spreading on their own typically require supplemental watering, fertilizer, and pesticide application to survive when used in landscapes and gardens. This maintenance costs you time and money. It can also cost wildlife. Because they need these additional supplements, exotic plants can contribute to pollution and the wasteful use of natural resources like water.

ESTABLISHING BALANCE IN YOUR YARD

Plants are the tools you are going to use to create your Backyard Wildlife Habitat garden or landscape. Native wildlife species have evolved to depend on the food and other habitat requirements provided by the plants that are also native to their ecosystem. The conditions that have shaped the native plant

◀ The eastern Flowering dogwood (*Cornus florida*), shown, and the western Pacific dogwood (*C. nuttallii*) are susceptible to an exotic fungus.

▼ Red-spotted purple butterfly alights on a black-eyed Susan (*Rudbeckia hirta* "Indian Summer").

▼ A backyard habitat in Maryland planted with native plants that hummingbirds and butterflies find attractive.

communities that naturally occur where you live include

- Soil moisture and nutrient level
- Sun and shade exposure
- Climate and precipitation patterns
- Relationship with the other plants and animals of the ecological community

Native plants are adapted to the range of seasonal conditions in their region. This means that they have evolved to take advantage of the amount of rain, weather and wind conditions, sunlight levels, and types of soil that occur naturally in a given area. Wildlife species evolved to take advantage of the resources provided by native plants. As a result, only native plants provide

the entire range of seasonal habitat benefits needed by native wildlife.

Native plants are great choices for your landscape. When planted in their natural conditions, they require almost no maintenance once they are established. While they are establishing themselves, native plants might need supplemental watering and mulching. It can take as little as a few weeks for natives to become established and rarely takes longer than one growing season. This can mean a significant reduction in the amount of pesticides and fertilizers released into the environment and can eliminate the need for supplemental watering.

With the knowledge of the components of a healthy ecosystem and an understanding of how your garden or landscape can play a role in restoring these components, you can make a difference for wildlife where you live by creating a habitat and certifying it with the National Wildlife Federation as a Backyard Wildlife Habitat site. You can start the process by learning more about the native wildlife in your area and how to provide the food, water, cover, and places for wildlife to raise young. The result will be a yard filled with the birds, butterflies, and other wildlife you wish to attract.

INFO ON NATIVE PLANTS

This book is for gardeners and wildlife enthusiasts in North America. When the term "native species" is used it refers to species native to North America. Few species have a native distribution over the entire continent, so consult with your state's native plant society, Natural Heritage program, natural resources agency, or local naturalists to determine which species naturally grow locally where you live. You can also visit the Lady Bird Johnson Wildflower Center's Website at http://www.wildflower.org/ for regional native plant lists, nurseries, landscapers, and other resources.

▲ Oregon grape (*Mahonia aquifolium*) is native to the western part of the United States.

chapter two

Providing Food for Wildlife

Food is the first component to consider for your wildlife habitat, and it is the one element that is most likely to attract wildlife to your yard or garden. You can offer food for wildlife in many different ways. Native plants provide the most natural source of food. Some wildlife will eat the plants or their fruit, or the plants may attract insects upon which other wildlife feeds. You can also supplement the natural food sources in a number of ways.

◄ Backyard wildlife, such as this eastern bluebird, rely on native plants and insects for food.

THE FOOD CHAIN

The food chain is a concept used to describe the process of how nutrients travel through the ecosystem and sustain wildlife. Plants capture energy from the sun, water, and minerals from the soil to create food for themselves in the form of carbohydrates. For this reason, plants are called producers and form the foundation of the food chain.

▲ This garden is filled with nectar-producing plants which feed many butterfly species.

Consumers are organisms that cannot create their own nutrients, but instead rely on producers and other consumers as food sources. All animals, including birds, mammals, fish, reptiles, amphibians, insects, and other invertebrates, are consumers. Some consumers rely solely on plants as their food source. These consumers are known as herbivores. Other consumers rely strictly on other animals for food. These consumers are known as carnivores (or in the case of consumers that feed primarily on insects and invertebrates, insectivores). Omnivores consume both plants and animals.

LINKS IN THE FOOD CHAIN

Every wildlife species provides a link in the food chain. As consumers eat plants and other animals, they transfer the energy from the sun and the nutrients manufactured by plants further along the food chain. Eventually, these nutrients end up in the body of an animal that has no natural predators. But this is not the end of the food chain. When the consumers at the top of the food chain eventually die, organisms called decomposers recycle the nutrients found in the bodies of consumers back into the raw materials needed by producers to make food. Decomposers also help break down dead plant material. Once the nutrients are returned to the soil, they are once again available for plants and the cycle begins anew.

The landscape you create can be a mini-ecosystem with multiple food chains. However, providing for wildlife is more than just putting out feeders. Your task is to provide the elements of the food chain and restore balance to the ecosystem. That may sound complicated, but it is simpler than you think. As a gardener, you are simply selecting which producers—native plants—will be part of your landscape. The producers provide for and attract the consumers, and the rest of the food chain falls into place. You can affect the types and numbers of wildlife species that you attract by your plant choices and garden design.

▶ Predators like this red-tailed hawk are important links in the food chain.

▶ The mountain ash (*Sorbus americana*) is an important wildlife food source.

▶ The black-tailed jackrabbit is a food source for predators such as hawks.

NATIVE TREES AND SHRUBS FOR BIRDS

Many different species of most of these types of trees and shrubs occur throughout North America. All provide fruit, seeds, or nuts that are relished by birds and other wildlife, and are ornamental. Visit NWF's Web site at www.nwf.org/gardenforwildlife for native plant resources.

- American beech (*Fagus grandifolia*)
- Aspen/Cottonwood (*Populus* spp.)
- Beautyberry (*Callicarpa americana*)
- Birch (*Betula* spp.)
- Blackberry (*Rubus* spp.)
- Blueberry (*Vaccinium* spp.)
- Cherry (*Prunus* spp.)
- Crabapple (*Malus* spp.)
- Currant (*Ribes* spp.)
- Dogwood (*Cornus* spp.)
- Elderberry (*Sambucus* spp.)
- Fir (*Abies* spp.)
- Fringe tree (*Chionanthus virginicus*)
- Hackberry (*Celtis occidentalis*)
- Hawthorn (*Crataegus* spp.)
- Holly (*Ilex* spp.)
- Juniper (*Juniperus* spp.)
- Mountain ash (*Sorbus scopulina*)
- Oak (*Quercus* spp.)
- Oregon Grape (*Mahonia* spp.)
- Pine (*Pinus* spp.)
- Sassafras (*Sassafras albidum*)
- Serviceberry (*Amelanchier* spp.)
- Spicebush (*Lindera benzoin*)
- Spruce (*Picea* spp.)
- Sumac (*Rhus* spp.)
- Tupelo (*Nyssa* spp.)
- Viburnum (*Viburnum* spp.)
- Wax-myrtle/Bayberry (*Myrica* spp.)
- Willow (*Salix* spp.)

PLANTS AS FOOD

Wildlife species native to your area have evolved with plants that are also native to that area. The best way to provide food for wildlife is to restore native plant communities in your yard. Plants provide food in a variety of ways. Some wildlife species eat the foliage and stems of plants, and some feed on plant sap. Others use berries and other fruits, nuts, seeds, nectar, and pollen as food.

Plants produce these foods specifically to attract wildlife. For example, flowers are brightly colored and fragrant not simply for human pleasure, but as a way of attracting hummingbirds, bats, butterflies, and other insects to the high-energy nectar within. The nectar itself is offered as a lure for these specialized species, called pollinators, to get them to brush against the reproductive parts of the plant and transfer pollen from one flower to the next to fertilize it. The fruits, berries, and nuts that are produced by fertilized flowers are little more than tasty and nutritious packages for a plant's indigestible seeds. Animals

digest the edible parts, pass the seeds through their digestive tracts, and deposit them far away from the parent plant, where they are ready to germinate.

USING NATIVE PLANTS

Some types of wildlife depend on only one type of native plant for survival. Monarch butterfly caterpillars can survive only on milkweed (*Asclepias* spp.). Many wildlife species can feed on a variety of different types of plants.

The landscape featured on this page has many different native plant species that will produce a variety of foods throughout the year. Some of the creatures that use these plant foods, notably insects, are themselves a crucial food source for other wildlife higher up on the food chain. Most birds, for example, feed their chicks exclusively or nearly exclusively on insects throughout the breeding season in the spring and into the summer. Come autumn, many birds again rely heavily on insects as a food source that helps fuel their migration.

▲ A certified Backyard Wildlife Habitat™ landscape can be attractive while providing a feast for wildlife.

◀ Native plants are the foundation of the food chain. Here a northern mockingbird feeds on the fruit of a red chokeberry (*Photinia pyrifolia*).

▲ A backyard habitat in Phoenix, AZ, is designed to attract hummingbirds. The plants are suited to the arid conditions of the area.

▼ The berries of this holly (*Ilex* spp.) provide a winter-time food source for a northern cardinal.

FOOD IN ALL SEASONS

You will have the most success in attracting a wide variety of wildlife to your yard or garden if you provide a mix of plants that, taken together, provide food throughout the year. Include some plants that bloom or put forth some food in spring, some that produce in summer, and others that produce in autumn and winter. This will ensure a steady availability of nectar, fruits, nuts, seeds, foliage, pollen, sap, and prey species throughout the year.

Providing food in autumn and winter is especially important. Species that go dormant or hibernate need to fatten up in the late summer and early autumn in order to survive winter. Migratory species need a steady source of food over a wide geographic range. Monarch butterflies are one of the few migratory insects. They rely on late-blooming plants such as asters (*Symphyotrichum* spp.) and goldenrods (*Solidago* spp.) to provide the nectar they need to make their journey south to Mexico or Southern California.

Keep the different components of the food chain in mind when you are planning your habitat. Do your planting plans include enough producers to feed the consumers you wish to attract in all seasons? Do you have a wide array of prey species for predatory consumers? Many songbirds, small mammals, and amphibians, for instance, are insectivores. If you kill all the insects, insectivorous wildlife species will lose their food source. Providing food at all levels of the food chain will ensure a thriving habitat filled with wildlife.

THE ROLE OF PREDATORS

Predators play an important role in the food chain. When predators are present, ecosystems tend to be more diverse, more resilient, and healthier. Predators help keep the ecosystem balanced by keeping the populations of those upon which they prey in check. Predators come in some surprising shapes and sizes and are a natural part of any ecosystem—including your backyard.

SPIDERS

Spiders on the whole catch and eat more insects—including most biting and plant-eating varieties—than all of the other insectivorous animals put together.

LADYBIRD BEETLES

Ladybird beetles, also known as ladybugs, have a voracious appetite for soft-bodied insects that feed on plants. Some species of ladybugs can eat about 5,400 aphids in a lifetime.

SALAMANDERS

All salamanders are carnivorous, eating insects, worms, slugs, and other invertebrates. The hatchlings of these amphibians are predators of mosquito larvae.

OWLS

Owls are incredibly silent in flight, aided by sound-suppressing fuzz that covers their flight feathers. They are able to rapidly locate and kill small mammals, birds, and insects in complete silence.

Other backyard predators that are commonly found throughout North America include dragonflies, damselflies, bats, foxes, and some types of snake.

SUPPLEMENTAL FEEDERS

The best way to provide food is to preserve and restore the local native plant communities that have supported wildlife for thousands of years. However, you can use feeders for some types of wildlife to supplement the natural food you provide through native plants. Providing feeders is also a great way to observe wildlife at a close range at a regular location.

▼ Feeders can supplement the food you provide through your plantings.

BIRD FEEDERS

Birds are one type of wildlife that can be safely fed with feeders. Studies have shown that birds rely on natural food sources first and use feeders only to supplement their diet. They won't become unnaturally dependent on feeders and won't delay seasonal migration or starve if you stop feeding them when you go on vacation.

Types of feeders. There are a variety of different types of bird feeders available. The most popular are tube feeders that can be filled with several seed types to attract different bird species. Platform feeders can be used for birds that normally forage on the ground and don't like to use a hanging feeder, such as mourning doves and many native sparrows. Hopper feeders have a roof and sides, typically hold a larger volume of seed, and often come in a variety of whimsical designs. Sock feeders made of fine mesh hold tiny seeds for birds such as goldfinches, while larger mesh can hold peanuts for species like blue jays, titmice, or Steller's jays. There are even feeders designed to hold insects or pieces of fruit for birds that don't normally eat seed or visit other types of feeders.

If you're installing a feeder, add grit to birdseed in the form of fine sand or crushed oyster shells or eggshells. (Bake the shells at 250 degrees for 20 minutes to kill any bacteria.) You can also maintain a bare sandy patch somewhere on your property, which many species will use as a source of grit. The grit not only aids in digestion; it also adds needed calcium to the bird's diet. This is especially important for females during the nesting season, who use the extra calcium to produce strong eggshells.

▲ The common tube feeder can be hung from a tree limb or mounted on a post.

▲ An eastern bluebird picks a mealworm from a feeder.

▼ There are many different types of feeders. Here, a Steller's jay feeds at a hanging tray feeder.

BEST SEEDS FOR FEEDERS

Different seed types will attract different species of birds to your feeder. Use seed types that are appropriate for your feeders. Black-oil sunflower will be eaten with relish by almost any bird species. Safflower is less appealing to squirrels and to exotic birds such as English sparrows.

- Black-oil sunflower
- Striped sunflower
- Sunflower hearts (hulled sunflower)
- Safflower
- Niger (also called thistle or nyger)
- Red millet
- White millet
- Cracked corn
- Peanuts (whole, shelled, or pieces)

31

▲ Suet is rendered animal fat that many birds species find hard to resist.

▶ Other critters will be drawn to suet feeders for a meal.

OTHER BIRD FOODS

▪ Mealworms

▪ Wax worms

▪ Raisins

▪ Currants

▪ Cherries

▪ Cranberries

▪ Grapes

▪ Grapefruit or orange halves

▪ Fruit jelly

▪ Peanut butter

▪ Sugar water "nectar"

▪ Popcorn

SUET FEEDERS

You can provide birds with a high-energy food source in winter by providing suet. Suet is rendered, or melted, animal fat. Suet feeders are wire cages that allow birds to cling to the wires and peck at the suet.

Suet is typically sold in square blocks sized to fit in standard suet feeders, and it can be purchased with a variety of additives such as dried fruit, seeds, and even dehydrated insects. You can make suet yourself by getting raw beef fat from a butcher, melting it, and then cooling it. (Be warned: this can be a very smelly

habitat hints:
BIRD FEEDING TIPS

- Store birdseed in a dry place. Moisture can cause mold to grow in seed, which can make birds sick.
- Clean out the feeder regularly to prevent disease. Use a stiff brush and hot water. You can use a mild detergent as long as you rinse the feeder thoroughly.
- Allow the feeder to dry completely before adding fresh seed.
- Keep the areas under the feeder raked clean. Seed shells and bird droppings can harbor illnesses, and spilled seed could attract pest species like Norway rats.
- Use feeders rather than spreading seeds on the ground, which can also attract pests.
- Don't overfeed. One or two feeders is fine, but more than that can cause unnatural crowding that can lead to stress, fighting, and spread of disease.
- If you have a problem with birds flying into your window, place the feeders closer to your house. Many birds hit windows when flying away from feeders.
- Keep feeders away from areas that provide cover for predators such as house cats.

See page 44 for tips on keeping squirrels out of feeders.

process.) You can use molds to create your own suet blocks sized to fit your suet feeder or use a casserole dish to create a large block from which you can slice smaller pieces to replenish your suet feeders as necessary. Store unused suet in the freezer.

Woodpeckers, nuthatches, creepers, and many other bird species including chickadees, titmice, and even hawks will eat suet if they can get it, especially in winter when other food sources are scarce. Other types of wildlife like suet as well. Tree squirrels and chipmunks will take advantage of suet feeders, and the occasional raccoon, opossum, or fox may clean up the scraps that fall to the ground.

▲ Many bird species will gather at a hopper feeder. Be sure to clean feeders and the area beneath them regularly.

▲ A female ruby-throated hummingbird hovers to feed at a nectar-producing plant.

▼ While Baltimore orioles enjoy nectar, you can also tempt them with feeders containing orange sections and grape jelly.

ATTRACTING HUMMINGBIRDS AND OTHERS

You can provide hummingbirds and other nectar-eaters like orioles with special feeders designed to simulate the flowers in which these birds naturally find the nectar they need to survive. You can purchase nectar mix, or you can make your own by boiling different concentrations of regular white sugar in water.

NECTAR RECIPE

To make homemade hummingbird nectar, boil one part sugar in four parts water. For orioles, boil one part sugar in eight parts water. Be sure to let your homemade nectar cool before offering it to birds. Orioles and some warblers will also feed on citrus fruit halves or grape jelly.

Never use honey or artificial sweeteners, as these are unhealthy for hummingbirds. Be sure to replace feeder nectar every two to three days, especially in warm weather, or it can go bad and make birds sick. You can refrigerate a batch of nectar for up to a week. After that, discard it and make a fresh batch. Hummingbirds are attracted to the color red, and many hummingbird feeders are red for this reason. However, putting red food coloring in your nectar isn't necessary. Planting red, tubular flowers is the most natural way of providing food for hummingbirds.

34

NECTAR PLANTS FOR HUMMINGBIRDS

Over 160 North American native plants are exclusively dependent upon hummingbirds for pollination. In the east, the ruby-throated hummingbird is the only species that commonly occurs. It is very territorial and will chase others away from feeders and flowers, so scatter these resources throughout your property to avoid competition. The 14 western species of humingbirds are less territorial and can be quite gregarious, and it's not an uncommon sight to find several different species sharing a single feeder.

Here are some North American native and nonproblematic exotic plants to attract hummingbirds:

- Beebalm (*Monarda didyma*)
- Cardinal flower (*Lobelia cardinalis*)
- Columbine (*Aquilegia* spp.)
- Coralbells (*Heuchera sanguinea*)
- Coral honeysuckle
  (*Lonicera sempervirens*)
- Fire pink (*Silene virginica*)
- Flowering tabacco (*Nicotiana* spp.)
- Fuchsia (*Zauschneria* spp.)
- Geiger tree (*Cordia sebestena*)
- Indian paintbrush
  (*Castilleja coccinea*)
- Jewelweed (*Impatiens capensis*)
- Mexican honeysuckle
  (*Justicia spicigera*)

- Penstemon (*Penstemon* spp.)
- Pineapple sage (*Salvia elegans*)
- Red buckeye (*Aesculus pavia*)
- Red yucca (*Hesperaloe parviflora*)
- Scarletbush (*Hamelia patens*)
- Scarlet morning glory
  (*Ipomoea cristulata*)
- Scarlet sage (*Salvia splendens*)
- Standing cypress (*Ipomoea rubra*)
- Sunset hyssop (*Agastache rupestris*)
- Tropical sage (*Salvia coccinea*)
- Trumpet creeper (*Campsis radicans*)
- Turk's cap mallow
  (*Malvaviscus arboreus*
  var. drummondii)

▲ Hummingbirds are naturally attracted to shades of red, such as the flowers of the beebalm plant.

Always keep in mind that while some birds may use feeders, almost all species require insects as a source of food for themselves and their young. This is even true of hummingbirds, which can't survive on nectar alone. Only about 25 percent of bird species will even use a feeder. Make sure you provide diverse native plant communities to support the year-round food needs of the birds that occur in your area.

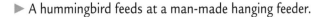

▶ A hummingbird feeds at a man-made hanging feeder.

FAMILY PROJECTS: EASY BIRD FEEDERS

You can make a variety of fun feeders for birds, squirrels, and other backyard wildlife. These edible feeders make great ornaments for your outdoor plants during holiday seasons or any time of the year. They are also great projects for kids.

WILDLIFE COOKIES

Suggested Materials:

■ Cookie cutters (stars, animals, etc.)

■ 1 loaf of white bread

■ 1 roll of ribbon

1 Use cookie cutters to punch shapes out of bread. Create a variety of shapes. 2 Use a pencil to poke a hole at the top of each cut out piece of bread for hanging. Leave the bread out overnight to harden. 3 Use ribbon or string to hang your ornaments outside around your yard.

WILDLIFE ENERGY MUFFINS

Suggested Materials:

- 1 cup chunky peanut butter
- 1 cup pure rendered suet or vegetable shortening
- 2½ cups coarse yellow corn meal
- Seeds, raisins, or other dried fruit and roasted peanuts
- Pipe clearners

1 Mix peanut butter, suet, and corn meal together. Stir in seeds, fruit, and nuts. 2 Make "muffins" by placing the mixture into a muffin tin. Sprinkle seeds on top. 3 Place a pipe cleaner in each muffin to act as a hanger, and place the tin in the freezer to harden. 4 Once hardened, hang the muffins from a tree.

FAMILY PROJECTS: EASY BIRD FEEDERS

PINECONE FEEDERS

Suggested Materials:

- ■ 1 cup chunky peanut butter
- ■ 1 cup pure rendered suet
- ■ 2½ cups coarse yellow cornmeal
- ■ 1 bag birdseed
- ■ 1 box of raisins
- ■ 1 roll of ribbon

1 Tie a length of ribbon to the base of the pinecone. Mix together peanut butter, suet, corn meal, 1 cup of birdseed, and ½ cup of raisins in a small bowl. 2 Stuff the mixture into each pinecone. 3 Roll pinecones in additional birdseed. 4 Hang from trees with string or ribbon.

BAGELS FOR THE BIRDS

Suggested Materials:

- 1 bag of plain bagels
- 1 jar of plain peanut butter
- 1 bag of birdseed
- 1 roll of ribbon

1 Split bagels lengthwise, and let them harden overnight.

2 Spread peanut butter over both sides of each bagel slice.

3 Sprinkle with birdseed. 4 Tie lengths of ribbon through each bagel hole, and hang bagels throughout your backyard.

FAMILY PROJECTS: EASY BIRD FEEDERS

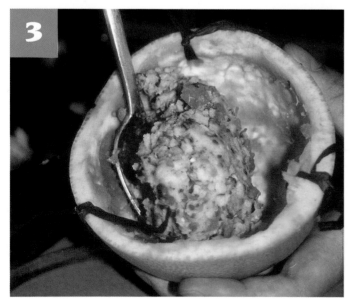

GRAPEFRUIT FEEDERS

Suggested Materials:

- 1 grapefruit (or orange)
- 2 pounds of suet
- 1 bag of birdseed
- 1 roll of string or ribbon

1 Cut grapefruit in half and hollow out. 2 Poke three holes in the edge of the grapefruit half that you are going to stuff. Tie string or ribbon through the holes, leaving 1 foot or more for hanging. 3 Stuff suet into the hollowed-out grapefruit half. 4 Sprinkle birdseed on suet. Place in the freezer to harden; then hang in yard.

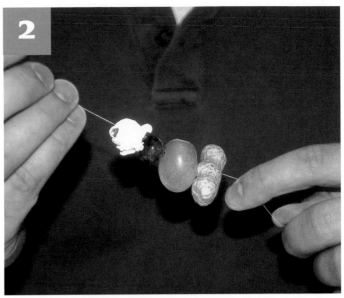

EDIBLE GARLAND

Suggested Materials:

- 1 roll of twine
- Sewing needles
- 2 bags of popped popcorn
- 3 bags of raw peanuts (in shells)
- 5 apples (cut into chunks)
- 2 bunches of grapes
- 2 bags of cranberries
- 4 oranges

1 Assemble all the ingredients before starting, and cut large pieces of fruit into sections. 2 Using the sewing needles, string items together, alternating between popcorn, apple chunks, grapes, cranberries, raw peanuts, and anything else you want to include.

3 Drape your garland around an evergreen tree or shrub. You can attach orange segments with red ribbon as highlights.

▶ The sight of a beautiful monarch butterfly feeding on goldenrod (*Solidago* spp.) would be a welcome find in any yard.

▼ This large butterfly garden contains nectar plants for adult butterflies, as well as host plants for their caterpillars.

BUTTERFLY FEEDERS

In addition to the nectar plants that are the primary natural food source for butterflies, you can purchase butterfly feeders that hold sugar solutions. As with hummingbird feeders, you can purchase nectar or make it yourself. Boil one part sugar in 18 parts water until the sugar dissolves; allow the solution to cool completely; and fill the feeder. Butterflies will also consume sports drinks like Gatorade®. You can put it into a feeder or simply pour some in a shallow dish and put in a sunny location. Again, be sure to change the sugar solution or sports drink every few days to prevent spoiling.

UNUSUAL DIETS

Some butterflies don't consume nectar at all but rather feed on tree sap, fermenting fruit, and even animal manure or carrion. This is especially true of woodland butterfly species like wood satyrs, wood nymphs, commas, and mourning cloaks. This presents some fun feeding opportunities and allows you to create a different kind of butterfly feeder. Begin by filling a shallow dish with fresh or overripe fruit—bananas, grapes, cantaloupes, apples, and pears are favorites, but just about any fruit will attract butterflies. Mash the skin so that the fruit oozes out. Birdbaths can easily be converted into butterfly feeders in this way. You can also hang fruit from shepherds' hooks or even impale fruit pieces on a nail in a fence. To make the fruit feeder even more attractive to these winged beauties, you can add a splash of sugar water, sports drink, beer, rum, or wine. (Remember, butterflies naturally consume fermenting fruit in the wild.)

▼ Come and get it. Overripe grapes attract a variety of butterflies, including hackberry emperor, tawny emperor, and red-spotted purple.

▼ A nail driven into a tree stump can anchor an ear of fresh or dried corn for feeding squirrels.

SQUIRREL FEEDERS

It's safe to feed squirrels, as long as you do it in moderation. There are over 250 species of squirrels worldwide that live everywhere from forests to deserts. Squirrels eat everything from seeds to nuts and plants, and some squirrels even eat insects, birds, and bird eggs. Providing squirrels with a feeder of their own can be one way of keeping them out of your bird feeders.

You can purchase a squirrel feeder at a birding specialty store or pet shop. To make one, hammer a long nail or screw through a piece of wood so that it sticks out at least 6 inches. Twist food onto the nail. Experiment with whole or chopped fruits and vegetables. Most squirrels love whole ears of fresh or dried corn. Smearing peanut butter on tree trunks in the early evening will attract nocturnal flying squirrels.

habitat hints:

KEEPING SQUIRRELS OUT OF BIRD FEEDERS

- Use a baffle, which is a piece of plastic or metal, that blocks the squirrel from the feeder. If the feeder is on a pole, add a baffle underneath the feeder. If the feeder is hung from a branch or if squirrels can drop onto the feeder from above, add a baffle on top of the feeder.
- Buy a feeder surrounded by screening that allows birds to get at the seed but blocks squirrels.
- Buy a feeder that uses gravity to close seed ports. Birds will be light enough to use the feeder, but the weight of a squirrel will close the seed ports.
- Feed safflower seed instead of sunflower. Safflower is less palatable to squirrels but is relished by many birds.
- Add cayenne pepper to your birdseed. Birds aren't affected by it, but squirrels will experience the nasty but harmless burning sensation. You can purchase seed premixed with cayenne.
- Learn to enjoy squirrels because no one has yet come up with a feeder or method that's perfectly squirrel-proof!

FEEDING OTHER SPECIES

Never feed any wildlife species human food scraps, trash, or even pet food. These types are unhealthy for most wildlife. Some species—mammals such as raccoons, skunks, bears, and deer, for example—can become dependent upon you and view humans as a source of food. When wildlife associates people with food, they can lose their natural fear of humans, and potentially dangerous close encounters can occur.

▲ Some wildlife species, such as deer, can become dependent on humans for food.

◀ If you wish to squirrel-proof your bird feeders, add a baffle around the pole. Or you can enjoy the squirrels that visit your feeders.

chapter three

Providing Water for Wildlife

All wildlife species need water for drinking and, in some cases, for bathing as well. For example, if birds can't bathe, their feathers become dirty, making flight difficult. Some species feed on aquatic or semiaquatic prey. In addition, water provides cover for a variety of wildlife, and many species need water to reproduce and as a place for their young to grow.

◄ Birds such as this northern cardinal need water for drinking and bathing.

PROVIDING WATER

There are many ways you can provide water in a Backyard Wildlife Habitat garden. The methods you choose will determine the type of wildlife attracted to your yard. Options range from water gardens to simple birdbaths. Even a muddy puddle will provide some wildlife with this necessary habitat element.

Do some research to learn about the different wildlife species in your area and how they depend on water. This research is important because each species of wildlife has unique water requirements. Water is found in a variety of forms in nature, and wildlife species in different areas have evolved to take advantage of these various water resources.

If you are planning to add a water resource to your yard, mimic the ways water would naturally occur there. This is important not only because local wildlife have adapted to use water in the way it naturally occurs but also because providing water in unnatural ways can have negative ecological consequences. Unnatural water features can support invasive exotic species that harm native species and can waste this important resource.

ADDING BIRDBATHS

Birdbaths can assist wildlife that have lost natural water sources as a result of overdevelopment, pollution, or drought. There are many models available in a wide variety of styles and materials. The best baths are relatively shallow with gradually sloping sides. A birdbath that is too deep or has sides that are too steep won't be as attractive to birds. A depth of 1 to 3 inches is best. You can place pebbles or a landing rock inside the birdbath to allow birds safe and easy access to the water. A bath made of plastic or similarly light material is usually easier to maintain and move. Concrete and metal are also good choices, but they may be heavy and difficult to move.

FAMILY PROJECT: BIRDBATH STUMP

You can create a simple, naturalistic water feature with nothing more than an old tree stump. Either a stump that is still rooted in the ground or a large log will work. You will also need a sharp chisel and some plants and rocks for the base of the birdbath. If you're working with children, be sure to keep them away from the chisel.

1 *If you're using a log, pick one that has a flat top and bottom and is at least 15 inches in diameter. Stand the log up on one end. An adult should use the chisel to tap out chunks of wood from the top of the log. The depression should be about 3 inches deep or less. Don't worry about making the depression smooth. Birds actually prefer a birdbath with rough surfaces, which keeps them from slipping when they land to drink or bathe.*

2 *If the log is large enough, add a rock on which birds can land, or place decorative pebbles in the bottom of the depression. You can change the pebbles whenever you wish. Visually anchor your stump with a few large stones at its base, and plant native ground cover. Your stump birdbath will become a focal point in the garden as well as a water resource for birds and other wildlife. Empty and refill the birdbath every few days.*

◀ A black-tailed jackrabbit drinks from a backyard wetland.

◀ American robins gather at a naturalistic birdbath.

◀ There are many types of birdbaths, such as the hanging type shown here.

▶ Birdbaths should be shallow with gradually sloping sides.

▲ Heated birdbaths make it easier for birds to take a drink during the winter.

▼ Add plants around a ground-level water source to create an attractive landscape feature.

In warm months when mosquitoes are active, you should empty and refill a birdbath every two to three days. This will prevent any mosquito larvae from metamorphosing into adults. Mosquitoes take three to five days to complete this process, so if you dump your bath more frequently than this, it will never produce adult mosquitoes. You should scrub out your birdbath periodically using a brush and mild detergent to remove droppings, feathers, dirt, and other debris.

Be careful to place your birdbath in an area near cover in case domestic cats or other predators appear, but not so close that these predators can use the cover to ambush birds and other critters coming for a drink. A distance of 10 to 12 feet is ideal.

If you choose, you can add a specially designed heater to your bath in the colder winter months. This helps birds who normally get liquid in the winter by eating snow. Most heated birdbaths don't use significant amounts of energy, and some are even solar heated. Another option is to purchase a heated dog water bowl, available at pet shops or farm supply stores. You can also simply remove the ice each day and refill the birdbath with fresh water.

PROVIDING GROUND-LEVEL WATER

A shallow dish placed on the ground will provide water for birds as well as wildlife such as rabbits and tortoises that can't fly or climb and therefore can't use a birdbath. Follow the same depth and cleaning specifications for a ground dish that you would for a birdbath. An on-the-ground dish also offers other opportunities for habitat. You can place a branch over the dish for a perch or create a small rock pile adjacent to the dish for critters to bask and hide. The dish itself will serve as a hiding place for insects and other invertebrates, as you'll learn when you lift it and see the many creatures scurrying for cover. These smaller wildlife species are a food source for birds and other insectivorous wildlife.

The same rules of placement, cover, and winter maintenance apply to this type of water feature. Birdbath dishes taken off their stand, flowerpot drainage pans, or even trash-can lids buried upside down can be used to create ground-level water features that will attract wildlife.

BIRDBATH MYTHS

Birds naturally get water in the winter by consuming snow or from moving streams, and they have no problem surviving without heated water provided by humans. Providing unfrozen water simply makes it easier for birds to get liquid without expending the extra body heat needed to melt snow. Feathers and feet will not freeze if they get wet in a birdbath, either.

▲ Many critters will find their way to ground-level water features.

▼ Placing a birdbath on the deck provides good wildlife viewing from the house.

PONDS AND WATER GARDENS

Ponds and water gardens are popular features that will be used by a variety of wildlife species if installed properly. Ponds can be large, natural bodies of water or smaller features that you add to your yard. Water gardens include smaller ponds, but the term also refers to container gardens that hold water and vegetation, such as half-barrels or even old bathtubs and water troughs.

EXISTING PONDS

In some areas ponds occur naturally while in others they are the result of human excavations. For example, one certified Backyard Wildlife Habitat owner in New Jersey purchased a house on two acres that were once part of a small family farm. The previous owner

◄ Native aquatic plants provide a source of food and cover for wildlife in addition to adding beauty to the landscape.

▼ Just about anything that can hold water, such as old bathtubs or whiskey barrels, can become a wildlife water feature.

had created a large berm at the back of the property to hold water flowing from a small spring on the other side of the property, resulting in the formation of a one-quarter acre pond.

REDOING THE POND

The current property owner planted native aquatic and emergent plants (vegetation that grows in wet soils), such as broadleaf cattail (*Typha latifolia*), pickerelweed (*Pontederia cordata*), and blue flag iris (*Iris versicolor*), among others. Perennials, shrubs, and trees that do well in wetland areas were added around the shoreline, such as cardinal flower (*Lobelia cardinalis*), Joe-pye weed (*Eupatorium fistulosum*), jewelweed (*Impatiens capensis*), swamp milkweed (*Asclepias incarnata*), crimson-eyed rosemallow (*Hibiscus moscheutos*), and alder (*Alnus* spp.). This shoreline area serves as buffer from the lawn and as a source of food and cover for wildlife. Great blue herons, mallard ducks, red-winged blackbirds, painted turtles, snapping turtles, green frogs, leopard frogs, spring peepers, northern water snakes, and several species of dragonflies and damselflies are just a few of the wildlife species that now call this pond

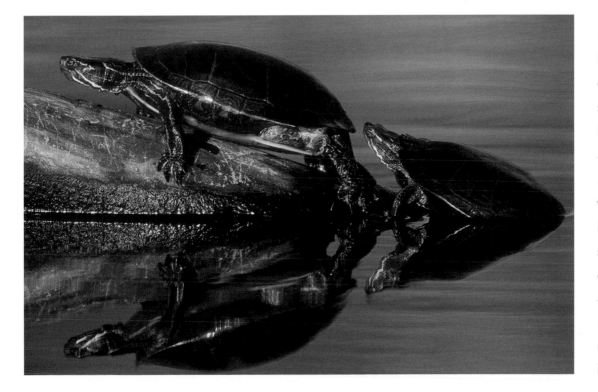

▲ A spicebush swallow tail lands on a cardinal flower, a species that does well in wet areas.

▲ Ponds can attract wildlife you never saw in your yard before, such as mallard ducks.

◄ Aquatic turtles need a place to bask in the sun.

53

PROJECT: ADDING A WILDLIFE POND

Earth-bottomed ponds allow the maximum opportunity for natural plant growth, and they offer places for wildlife to hibernate in the mud and debris at the bottom. But in most places, if you simply dug a hole and filled it with water, the water would seep into the ground. Even in areas with high-clay-content soils, water will eventually percolate down. To prevent water from being absorbed by the earth, install either a preformed hard plastic or flexible sheet liner.

TOOLS & MATERIALS

- 1 garden hose or spray paint
- Shovels, picks, and other digging tools
- 1 4-foot level
- 1 straight 2x4 long enough to span hole
- 1 pool liner and pond pump
- Pond plants

1 *Pick a location for your new pond. Use a garden hose to outline the area where you'd like the finished pond to be. You can use spray paint to "draw" the outline as well. The depth of the pond will depend on your region and which wildlife species you wish to attract. The colder the climate, the deeper the pond needs to be to accommodate aquatic wildlife year-round. In most places a depth of 30 inches is sufficient to ensure that the pond doesn't freeze entirely, killing fish, hibernating reptiles, amphibians, and other aquatic wildlife. Extremely cold areas will require a depth of 4 feet.*

2 *Plan the underwater topography by sketching a cross section of what you want your pond to look like under water. Plan for a variety of levels and shelves at different depths. Include a wide, shallow area on one side that will allow wildlife such as amphibians to enter and exit easily. Birds will also use the shallow section to drink and bathe. Sketching your ideas on paper before actually digging will allow you to experiment with different designs. Once you've settled on a design plan, determine the specific depth and slope of each shelf to guide you as you dig.*

3 The shape of your wildlife pond should be natural and undulating instead of rigid and symmetrical. Use a level and a 2 x 4 to ensure that the perimeter is level from edge to edge, otherwise water will spill out of the lower side. Once you've dug the hole according to plan, carefully rake the soil in the hole as smooth as you can, removing any rocks or other jagged debris that could potentially tear the liner. Adding a layer of smooth sand as a buffer is a good idea as well.

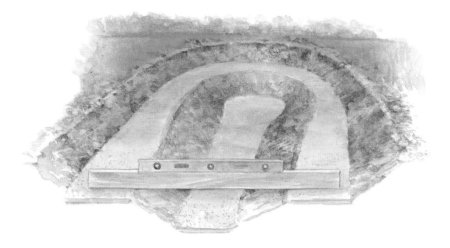

4 Unroll the liner in a warm, sunny spot to make it more pliable, and then place it over the hole. Press it against the ground in the hole with your hands, molding it to the shape of the shelves. There will be some wrinkles and creases that look unattractive in the empty pond, but once the pond is filled with water and plants, you won't be able to see them. Be sure to overlap the liner at least 8 inches around the edge of the pond to prevent the water from draining under the liner if the pond floods during a heavy rain. Place decorative rocks around the edge to hide the liner and hold it in place.

5 Add a pump and plants, and then sit back and wait for the wildlife to arrive. You won't have long to wait! You can also jump-start your pond ecosystem by adding a couple of bucketfuls of water and leaf debris from a nearby pond. Make the shoreline more accessible to wildlife by placing stacked rocks, logs, or branches that dip into the water. These will be used by wildlife as "ladders" to enter and exit the pond. Native vegetation in and around the pond will also help wildlife get in and out, and it will provide food, cover, and places to raise young as well. Aquatic plants need to be potted, since they will not be able to root themselves into the plastic liner.

▲ Aquatic plants will help keep algae in check.

▶ Spicebush swallowtails enjoy puddling on damp soil.

▶ Vegetation helps wildlife enter and exit container gardens.

POND FEATURES

In most cases a simple pump is needed to circulate and aerate the water. You can also install a fountain or create a waterfall feature. Birds, in particular, are attracted to the sound of moving or trickling water. Many different-sized pumps made specifically for water gardens are available commercially. If you don't have an appropriate electrical outlet nearby, you'll need to work with an electrician to have a GFCI receptacle, which is the type necessary for outdoor locations, installed. The bigger the pond, the bigger the pump you'll need. For smaller ponds, you can purchase a solar-powered pump that won't require any electrical work.

DEALING WITH ALGAE

Algae blooms often occur in newly established ponds. This is a normal part of the process as microorganisms develop that will become the "biological filter" for the pond. Once established, aquatic vegetation will outcompete algae for light and nutrients and prevent excessive algae blooms. It normally takes new ponds six to eight weeks to find their balance once other plants are added. Monitor nutrient load in the pond to prevent continued algae blooms. Don't let any fertilizer get into the water from the surrounding landscape. If you must fertilize aquatic plants, use pellets designed for that specific purpose. Don't overstock your pond with fish, and don't overfeed them. (Fish waste and uneaten food promote excess algae.) Bales of organic barley straw purchased from a commercial water garden specialist can also be added to the pond to reduce algae blooms.

Once your pond is established, allow a moderate amount of dead leaves and debris to accumulate on the bottom. These areas will be used as breeding and hiding places for aquatic invertebrates as well as reptiles, amphibians, and amphibian larvae. If your pond is deep enough and has enough submerged debris, some amphibian and reptile species may also use it as a hibernation area.

You can purchase a heater for your pond to keep it ice-free in winter. As with birdbath heaters, pond heaters simply keep the water just above freezing and typically don't require a large amount of electricity. Pond heaters are not crucial, especially if your pond is the appropriate depth for the region.

CONTAINER WATER GARDENS

Water gardens can be created using any number of containers to hold water and plants. When creating water gardens, keep wildlife use in mind. Water troughs, half-barrels, or any other container deeper than 3 inches can trap wildlife that falls into the relatively deep water, unless vegetation or some other exit point is present. Songbirds typically won't use this type of water feature either. You can make your water garden more wildlife-friendly by adding potted water plants or branches or even by filling the container with rocks to serve as "islands."

PUDDLES AND MUDDY AREAS

You can create another type of water feature that might seem a little strange: a mud puddle. Butterflies, males in particular, can often be seen engaging in a behavior called "puddling." When they find a wet, muddy patch of soil or even fresh animal manure, they gather and lap up the liquid, which is rich in minerals. You can create your own puddling area by filling a shallow pan with sand mixed with some soil or manure, filling it with water, and placing it in a sunny area.

▲ Pitcher plants (*Sarracenia* spp.), which grow in nutrient-poor bogs, trap insects for nutrients.

▼ The sundew plant (*Drosera* spp.) is acclimated to growing in acidic peat bogs.

WETLAND HABITATS

Wetland areas occur naturally where the topography of the land causes water to collect and pool. Wetland areas typically drain off into a stream, river, or lake and are often only seasonally inundated with water. There are many different types of natural wetlands. A swamp is a wooded wetland. A marsh is a wetland that does not support trees and is characterized by grasses, sedges, rushes, and other herbaceous plants adapted to saturated soils and standing water. Vernal pools, wet meadows, wet prairies, and prairie potholes are all types of wetlands that collect standing water from precipitation but typically dry out during the summer or dry season. A bog is a type of wetland in which plant material has accumulated faster than it can decompose and formed a substrate called peat. Bogs are usually very acidic and poor in nutrients. Carnivorous plants, like sundew (*Drosera* spp.), pitcher plant (*Sarracenia* spp.), butterwort (*Pinguicula* spp.), and Venus flytrap (*Dionaea muscipula*) often grow in bogs. Their ability to lure and trap insect prey as a nutrient source is an adaptation to living in nutrient-deprived bogs.

CREATING WETLAND GARDENS

You can create your own wetland garden by mimicking natural wetlands. You can divert storm runoff from your roof or from a basement sump pump into an area planted with wetland species. You can also plant wetland species in any area that naturally collects water in your yard. A rain garden is a type of wetland garden that mimics a natural wet meadow or prairie. Rain gardens are planted in a location specifically to block and absorb water and nutrients that would otherwise wash off your yard into storm drains after it rains. There are native plants adapted to wet conditions in most regions that will thrive in a wet area in your yard. Wetland gardens like these will provide wildlife habitat and reduce runoff.

MOVING WATER

Moving bodies of water—streams, rivers, and creeks—provide habitat for different wildlife species than those found in ponds

PROJECT: STORMWATER WETLAND

The National Wildlife Federation's chief naturalist Craig Tufts created a stormwater wetland in his yard. He offers these tips:

- As with any project involving significant landscape change, check with your homeowners' association and municipal government to make sure your intended wetland project is permissible.

- Talk with your neighbors. A wetland garden such as a stormwater marsh or rain garden will look quite different from a lawn.

- Choose a site based on access to water and that is flat enough to support a wetland. Using roof runoff to supply water is a good idea, since gravity will work in your favor to bring water to the wetland and because the water quality tends to be good.

- Base your site selection on the kinds of plants you want to grow. For example, if you want to grow sun-loving plants, choose a sunny location on the south side of your home.

- A third consideration is soil type. Very sandy soil is too permeable to adequately hold water. Soil with a good deal of absorbent clay works well.

**CROSS-SECTION
FULL SUN VERSION**

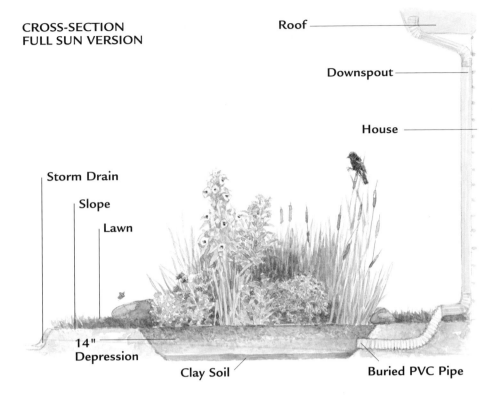

INSTALLATION

 Outline the perimeter of the proposed site.

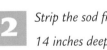 Strip the sod from the outlined area, and excavate the subsoil and rock to about 14 inches deep. You will also need to dig a trench connecting the growing area to the downspout of the house.

 During excavation, use a level to make sure the ground is even.

 Connect a length of flexible plastic pipe to a downspout from the roof, angling it away from the house and burying it beneath the ground and into the wetland. Make sure the angle of the pipe is great enough to avoid water backup during a big storm.

 Prepare the soil. If your soil is very clayey, work sand, compost, and other organic material into the top few inches.

 Choose native wetland plants that provide food, cover, and places to raise young for wildlife.

or lakes. Many fish species are adapted to the oxygen-rich waters of cold, fast-moving streams. Swift currents mean wildlife living in these areas must have body shapes and habits that prevent them from being swept away in the rushing water. Chunky-bodied amphibian species that live in ponds, such as bullfrogs, are replaced by streamlined species such as salamanders.

If you're lucky enough to have a moving water feature naturally occurring on your property, protect it from erosion and other runoff with a buffer of native vegetation.

ADDING A MOVING WATER FEATURE

If your property has a slope, you can create your own moving water feature using the same types of pump and flexible plastic liner that you'd use to create a small pond. Create a small pond area at the bottom of the slope, and then run flexible piping to the top of the slope. Dig a long, curving "stream-bed" depression, and line it with flexible pond liner. Cover the streambed with gravel and randomly placed larger stones, and add streamside plants. Finally, pump the water from the lower pond up to the top, where it will run down the stream bed and create a wonderful moving water habitat.

BULLFROGS IN THE WEST

The American bullfrog is native to the eastern and central parts of the United States and Canada. It has been widely introduced outside its range, however, and has become a problematic invasive exotic in the West. It consumes other frogs such as the endangered Chiricahua leopard frog native to Arizona, New Mexico, and Mexico.

Never purchase and release into the wild tadpoles or frogs from mail-order science supply catalogs or from pet shops. Chances are that they are not native to your area, and they could become invasive or spread disease to wild populations. A better way to experience these creatures is to create habitat and let native amphibians come on their own.

▲ American bullfrogs have become invasive in some western states and Mexico.

SHORELINE HABITAT

If you're lucky enough to own property adjacent to a large, natural body of water, whether it's a lake, river, or coastal area, there are some unique habitat opportunities for you. Your goal should be to maintain the natural vegetative or geologic buffers that naturally protect the water from chemical runoff and erosion. In addition to protecting these bodies of water, buffer areas provide habitat for a variety of creatures.

Rivers and lakes naturally have vegetation down to their shores or beach areas. If you have a mowed lawn, try to leave a swath of vegetation 10 to 12 feet wide along the shore. Large ponds, lakes, and rivers often naturally have fallen logs and other woody debris extending from the shoreline. This woody debris provides an important basking area for turtles and other semiaquatic reptiles and amphibians. They are also used as hunting perches by wading birds.

HABITAT FOR AQUATIC SPECIES

Below the surface of the water, the branches create a maze of chambers and crevices for hiding and hunting. Freshwater fish and other aquatic species use these areas of fallen woody debris in much the same way that oceanic species use coral reef structures and terrestrial creatures use brush piles. Fallen woody debris also slows the current, which prevents erosion and creates resting, feeding, and hiding places for aquatic species. For example, the removal of fallen woody debris from many Pacific Northwest streams and rivers has proven disastrous for several salmon species that need the slower-moving pools that such areas create as safe hiding and feeding places for young. If you have fallen woody debris in your body of water, leave it in place. If no woody debris is present, consider adding a large log, a fallen snag, or even a tangle of branches.

PAMPAS GRASS

INVADER OF CALIFORNIA COAST

Showy South American native pampas grass (*Cordateria selloana*) has been sold as an ornamental since 1848. Its pale buff colored plume is very attractive and can make a bold visual statement in a landscape. Unfortunately, it has escaped cultivation is now invading California coastal areas, destroying habitat of native coastal plants and wildlife.

◄ You can create a waterfall with a pond pump and flexible PVC piping.

▼ Create a native plant buffer around shoreline to keep lawn runoff out of the water.

MAINTAINING YOUR WATER FEATURE

While you're deciding on the type of water source you'd like to provide for wildlife, consider the amount of maintenance that will be required to keep it clean. If you allow your water source to become dirty, it could be harmful to wildlife. Smaller, shallow water sources can easily be polluted by animal waste and need to be emptied and washed often. For water gardens, plants provide food, cover, and places for wildlife to raise young, but they will also serve as natural filters of animal waste and excess nutrients. Purchasing a pump-driven filter is also a possibility, though not a necessity.

As mentioned earlier, mosquitoes need about three to five days to complete their metamorphosis from aquatic larvae into winged adults. If you dump your bird-bath or shallow water pan every two to four days, mosquitoes will never be able to reach the point of metamorphosis. Ponds, water gardens, and wetland areas will have a wide variety of mosquito predators that will help keep populations in check.

Many water-gardening enthusiasts collect koi or ornamental goldfish as well. While there is nothing wrong with this aspect of the hobby, goldfish, koi, and other ornamental fish don't fit into a natural water feature for wildlife. Koi and

◀ Well-maintained water features attract a host of mosquito predators.

▶ Empty and refill bird baths and other water features regularly.

WEST NILE VIRUS

Having a water feature for wildlife does not put you at increased risk of contracting West Nile virus if you follow some simple precautions. Less than one percent of people infected with West Nile virus actually develop symptoms. On the other hand, 140 bird species have been affected. Some species have experienced very high mortality rates.

WEST NILE FACTS AND TIPS

- West Nile virus first appeared in New York in 1999 and has since spread across the United States and into Mexico and Canada.

- Avoid peak times of mosquito activity; use insect repellent; and wear long pants and sleeves.

- Help control mosquito breeding by cleaning gutters and regularly draining the saucers under flowerpots, wading pools, and other objects that collect water in your yard. Change the water in birdbaths, wildlife water sources, and pet dishes frequently.

- Insecticide spraying to control mosquitoes may have other serious harmful effects. More research is needed to understand the impact of West Nile virus on wildlife, the ecological repercussions of spraying insecticides in wetlands, and the potential for human vaccines.

goldfish are native to Asia, and in some cases when they've escaped or been released from captivity, these exotics have had a negative impact on native wildlife. If you do have exotic fish, be sure that they have no means of escape into natural waterways, and never deliberately release these species into the wild. Adding such fish into a pond in a wildlife-friendly landscape could be an unwise investment; koi in particular are very expensive and so brightly colored that they are often an easy catch for native fish predators like herons and raccoons.

AVOIDING UNWANTED CHEMICALS

Birds, reptiles, amphibians, and other aquatic wildlife are extremely susceptible to pesticides. Be careful what you put on your lawn and garden, as it may wash into your water feature.

Even if you don't use chemicals in your yard, you might be adding them when you top off your pond. In most municipalities, chlorine is added to tap water to kill microorganisms that could be unhealthy for humans. Recently a new chemical, chloramine, has been used because it persists in the water longer than chlorine. Both can harm amphibians and the microorganisms in the water. Fortunately, chlorine evaporates out of tap water within 24 hours. If you need to add significant amounts of water to your water garden, fill several buckets and let them sit for a day before adding to your pond. You can also purchase water conditioner from a pet shop or water-garden supply company that will neutralize chlorine and chloramine instantly.

chapter four

Providing Cover for Wildlife

Many species rely on cover, or shelter, to provide protection from the elements as well as from predators. At the same time, predators rely on cover to camouflage and conceal themselves in order to successfully stalk or ambush their prey. While you should remove cover that allows non-native predators, such as house cats, to attack wildlife, providing cover for natural predators contributes to a well-balanced backyard habitat.

◀ A densely planted landscape provides wildlife species with cover from predators and the elements.

PROVIDING NATURAL COVER

Restoring natural cover features in your yard is the best way to provide this important habitat element for wildlife. There are a variety of ways in which wildlife species find cover in the wild, and there are just as many different ways you can provide it in your yard or garden.

NATIVE PLANTS AS COVER

In the same way that native plant communities provide the best and most sustainable food source for wildlife, they also provide the best form of cover. Because wildlife species evolved with native plant communities, their life cycles and cover needs are in tune with the seasonal changes of native plants. Any native plant community will provide natural cover for the wildlife species that are also native to the region.

No matter which plants you choose, plant them in a way that mimics the natural structure that native plants form in the wild. For example, forest plant communities have several different structural "layers," from the forest floor all the way up to the treetop canopy. Each of these layers supports different wildlife species. If you have large mature trees, add an understory layer of smaller tree species and large shrubs. This understory can then be underplanted with smaller shrubs, woodland wildflowers, sedges, and ferns. In doing so, you provide several new layers of cover and will support many more wildlife species.

▲ A Carolina wren seeks cover in the dense branches of a fir tree.

◄ Provide cover by mimicking nature. Here underplantings complement the tree.

habitat hint:
TIPS FOR PLANTING A WILDLIFE SHRUB ROW

A wildlife shrub row is a densely planted row of woody plants made up of a variety of different native species. Wildlife species will hide within and use the shrub row as a sheltered path as they move across the landscape.

- Select shrubs with varying mature heights to add visual interest.
- Select plant species that have flowers or berries that wildlife can use as food sources.
- Plant densely to provide the most cover, but keep the mature size of your plants in mind to limit overcrowding. For medium-sized shrubs, planting about 5 feet apart is good spacing.
- Use your shrub row to connect two naturally planted or wild areas that are separated by lawn or other open space. Your shrub row will then be used as a corridor.
- To provide the most cover, allow your shrubs to grow according to their natural branching structures rather than pruning them back or into geometric shapes.
- If you have bird feeders or birdbaths, place them about 10 to 12 feet from your shrub row. This is close enough that birds can escape to the shrub row if a cat appears but not so close that the cat will be able to use the shrub row as a hiding place from which to ambush the birds.
- A wildlife shrub row planted along your property line will also serve as a living fence.
- Plant diversely to provide for the widest range of wildlife. A good native shrub row recipe is one evergreen species, two nectar-producing species, two berry-producing species, and one thorny species. The quantity of each species depends on available space.
- Plant native wildflowers and grasses in front of your shrub row to add more habitat and create a finished look to the shrub row.

▲ Shrub rows provide cover for wildlife species, and the flowers and berries are an important food source.

▲ Typical species used to re-create a grass-land meadow.

▲ Native grasses and wildflowers provide excellent cover.

Different native plants offer different types of cover. Plants that have dense growth patterns provide more cover from both weather and predators. Plants that have thorns on their leaves or branches add yet another layer of cover that will allow smaller creatures a safe escape from larger predators. Evergreen species also provide excellent cover, especially in areas subject to cold temperatures. There are evergreen plant species native to most areas.

GRASSLANDS AS COVER

Grassland plant communities provide excellent cover for a wide range of wildlife species, from insects and birds to small and large mammals. As their name suggests, grasslands comprise mainly grass species; their close relatives, the sedges; scattered wildflowers; and in some areas shrubs and the occasional tree.

(A grassland with scattered trees and shrubs is called a savannah.) Grasslands naturally occur over a wide range of the North American continent, from the southwestern desert grasslands of California and the Southwest, to the sagebrush steppe in the Intermountain West, to the prairie communities of the Great Plains. Native grasslands have largely been turned into agricultural crop or grazing land or, increasingly, water-thirsty lawns composed of exotic grass species.

The Great Plains is the largest grassland ecosystem in the U.S., stretching from the Appalachian Mountains in the East to the Rocky Mountains in the West, and it consists of three distinct plant communities. Eastern tallgrass prairie occurs in areas with significant rainfall and supports grasses over 5 feet tall. Western shortgrass prairie occurs in arid areas in the shadow of the Rockies and supports grasses that grow 2 feet or less. Mixed-grass prairie occurs where tallgrass transitions into shortgrass and supports grass species that grow between 2 and 5 feet. Meadows occur in areas with significant rainfall that supports the growth of woody plants and sprout where the tree cover has been disturbed. If meadows are not managed, they are eventually shaded out as trees return.

Even a small patch of native grasses and wildflowers will provide cover for a variety of creatures. Restoring these types of plant communities is another way you can provide needed cover in your yard naturally.

INVASIVE EXOTIC SHRUBS

The following exotic shrubs and small trees are invasive in parts of North America and should not be planted. Most are still commonly available for sale in nurseries. In the past, some were touted for their wildlife value because birds will feed on their berries. But when birds eat the fruit, they also spread the seeds, allowing these shrubs to invade and degrade diverse native plant communities that support many other species of wildlife.

- Amur honeysuckle (*Lonicera maackii*)
- Autumn olive (*Elaeagnus umbellata*)
- Brazilian pepper (*Schinus terebinthifolius*)
- Burning bush (*Euonymus alatus*)
- Chinese privet (*Ligustrum sinense*)
- Cotoneaster (*Cotoneaster* spp.)
- European privet (*Ligustrum vulgare*)
- European buckthorn (*Rhamnus cathartica*)
- Glossy buckthorn (*Rhamnus frangula*)
- Japanese barberry (*Berberis thunbergii*)
- Japanese privet (*Ligustrum japonicum*)
- Japanese spiraea (*Spiraea japonica*)
- Morrow honeysuckle (*Lonicera morrowii*)
- Multiflora rose (*Rosa multiflora*)
- Nandina/Heavenly bamboo (*Nandina domestica*)
- Russian olive (*Elaeagnus angustifolia*)
- Scotch broom (*Cytisus scoparius*)
- Tartarian honeysuckle (*Lonicera tatarica*)

▲ The berries of invasive Japanese barberry (*Berberis thunbergii*).

69

THE IMPORTANCE OF DEAD VEGETATION

Even dead and dying plants can provide cover. Leave the dead stems of herbaceous plants standing until spring after the flowers and leaves have died back. The fruits and seeds that develop from flowers will become a food source, while the stalks provide an extremely important cover source for a variety of insects. (These insects are an important food source for wildlife higher up on the food chain.) Similarly, woody debris, such as rotting logs on the ground, provides an important source of cover for many insects and other invertebrates, as well as for small mammals, salamanders, and even some snake species. Dead standing

NATIVE VINES

These ornamental vines are native to different parts of North America, and all provide cover for wildlife. Some also offer nectar for hummingbirds and insects; others provide berries for birds and mammals; and some are even host plants for butterfly caterpillars.

- American wisteria (*Wisteria frutescens*)
- Carolina jessamine (*Gelsemium sempervirens*)
- Clematis (*Clematis* spp.)
- Coral honeysuckle (*Lonicera sempervirens*)
- Crossvine (*Bignonia capreolata*)
- Dutchman's pipe (*Aristolochia* spp.)
- Greenbriar (*Smilax* spp.)
- Orange honeysuckle (*Lonicera ciliosa*)
- Passionflower (*Passiflora* spp.)
- Pepper vine

- (*Ampelopsis arborea*)
- Poison ivy (*Rhus radicans*)*
- Pride-of-California (*Lathyrus splendens*)
- Trumpet creeper (*Campsis radicans*)
- Twining snapdragon (*Maurandella antirrhiniflora*)
- Virginia creeper (*Parthenocissus quinquefolia*)
- Wild grape (*Vitis* spp.)

Note: If you aren't allergic to poison ivy, keep what grows on your property. Over 60 species of birds and mammals consume its berries.

INVASIVE VINES

Many commonly occurring vines are invasive exotic species. Some were accidental introductions, but most were brought to North America as ornamentals or for erosion control. Do not purchase these species, and try to remove those already in the landscape:

- Chinese wisteria (*Wisteria sinensis*)
- Climbing euonymus (*Euonymus fortunei*)
- English ivy (*Hedera helix*)
- Fiveleaf akebia (*Akebia quinata*)
- Japanese honeysuckle (*Lonicera japonica*)
- Japanese wisteria (*Wisteria floribunda*)
- Kudzu (*Pueraria montana*)
- Mile-a-minute (*Polygonum perfoliatum*)
- Oriental bittersweet (*Celastrus orbiculatus*)
- Porcelainberry (*Ampelopsis brevipedunculata*)

trees are called snags. Snags occur naturally in forest plant communities and are an extremely valuable source of cover. As trees age, branches break off and holes begin to form. These cavities are used by many birds and mammals as important nesting areas as well as for cover. Leave snags standing in the landscape whenever possible, as long as they pose no danger of falling and damaging people or property. Rather than completely removing the snag as decay progresses, you can minimize any potential hazard by pruning off the more rotten limbs or even the entire top portions of the snag. You can dress up a snag by planting native flowering vines at its base.

◀ Ring-necked snakes find shelter under fallen woody debris where they feed on worms and slugs.

▼ Fallen trees, such as the one shown here, provide cover for wildlife.

71

▲ Water features, such as this pond, provide cover for aquatic species.

WATER AS COVER

Water is the second natural way of providing cover for wildlife. Many creatures, in particular many reptile and amphibian species, need bodies of water at least a few feet deep in order to escape predators. Green frogs, bullfrogs, southern pig frogs, and western spotted frogs are just a few of the species that dive into the water and hide in the mud and leaf litter at the first sign of danger.

Basking aquatic turtles also dive for the protective cover of water, and stay submerged until the danger has passed. Painted turtles, western pond turtles, and the many species of map turtles, river cooters, and sliders are common species that exhibit this behavior. Some turtle species spend most of their time hiding below the water's surface and rarely leave their aquatic cover except to lay eggs. Musk turtles, snapping turtles, and spiny softshell turtles all behave this way. All of the frogs and turtles mentioned use water as a source of cover to ambush their prey, which includes insects, fish, other amphibians and reptiles, and for the larger species, even birds and small mammals.

By adding or restoring water features to the landscape, you'll be providing cover for a great range of aquatic and semiaquatic species—predators and prey alike.

NATURAL CAVITIES

Natural cavities can be found in rock or in the ground just as they are found in trees. These cavities are also an important source of cover for many species of wildlife and should be protected and preserved. The many species of chipmunks and mole salamanders find cover in natural crevices and tunnels below the ground. Some mole salamander species emerge from these places for only a few days a year to mate, and then return underground. Filling in natural dens and burrow sites can evict many species of wildlife that depend upon them. Woodchucks, black-tailed prairie dogs, and the endangered gopher tortoise all excavate tunnels in the ground that many other wildlife species need as a source of cover.

▲ A red-phase screech owl uses a natural cavity in a tree for cover.

◄ Burrowing owls find cover in underground cavities.

73

HUMAN-MADE COVER

You can also provide cover by building or purchasing cover features. These human-made cover features can be made of artificial materials or natural ones, and they simply replicate forms of cover that occur naturally.

▲ A brush pile will become a "wildlife hotel."

▼ A white-throated sparrow finds shelter in a brush pile.

CREATING LOG AND BRUSH PILES

You can create the type of cover that naturally occurs when trees fall and dead wood accumulates on the ground by building a log or brush pile. Log piles are simply stacks of cut wood. If you have a fireplace, you probably already have a log pile that's providing hiding places for many small animals. Brush piles are made up of a variety of different sizes of wood and are less formal looking than a log pile. When built correctly, a brush pile can house creatures as large as foxes and as small as insects like the mourning cloak butterfly, which will hibernate as an adult in a brush pile. Birds such as wrens find both cover and places to hunt their insect prey in brush piles, and may even nest there. Be sure to check with your homeowners' association or local building department to find out whether there are any ordinances against having brush piles. Building these woody wildlife hotels is also a great way to keep fallen yard debris out of the landfill.

ADDING ROCK FEATURES

You can create similar structures made out of rock. A rock pile can be as small or as large as you like, depending on the space and the rock with which you have to work. As with a brush pile, start with larger rocks at the bottom of the pile and add progressively smaller pieces. You can add pieces of PVC piping in the interior of your rock pile to create larger tunnels hidden by

FAMILY PROJECT: CREATE A BRUSH PILE

Although they may look like random piles of sticks and logs, it is important to build brush piles according to a specific plan in order to provide effective cover for wildlife.

1 *Place fireplace-size or larger logs on the ground about 12 to 15 inches apart. This will allow spaces for larger wildlife. Then take smaller branches, up to about 2 inches in diameter, and start criss-crossing them on top of the larger pieces.*

2 *Continue stacking wood in this manner. Add evergreen branches towards the top of the pile to add even more cover. If you're concerned about the look of the brush pile, plant a flowering vine to grow over the top of it.*

3 *The finished brush pile should be about 5 feet in diameter at the base, shaped like a dome with larger cavities in the interior near the bottom, and with a maze of progressively smaller spaces toward the outside of the pile.*

the exterior rock. Loose-laid rock walls are simply narrow rock piles used as a border. Like shrub rows, rock walls will serve as places of escape for wildlife as well as sheltered corridors. Mortared rock walls do not provide the cover wildlife needs.

Rock features are particularly attractive to creatures that depend on their surrounding environment for temperature regulation. If you place your rock feature in a sunny area, it will absorb heat during the day and slowly release it during the cool evenings. Reptiles, such as skinks or horned lizards, and many butterfly species will bask in the morning sunlight after a chilly night or absorb heat radiating from the rocks in the evening as temperatures drop. In desert landscapes, rock features can play an important role from a landscape design perspective, adding visual interest and regional character.

▲ The nooks and crannies in a rock wall will shelter many species.

▲ A flying squirrel shelters in a roosting box.

HOUSES FOR CRITTERS

INSTALLING ROOSTING BOXES

Roosting boxes provide protection for birds and small mammals during cold or harsh weather. By grouping close together in the enclosed space of a roosting box, the wildlife present generates warmth.

Different species use roosting boxes at different times of the year, so be sure to take the time to observe what is coming and going from your roosting box—you wouldn't want to miss a special wildlife viewing opportunity.

There are a variety of houses designed to provide cover for specific wildlife or groups of wildlife. Some critter houses are made commercially and can be purchased at your local garden store, at nature centers, or through catalog companies. You can also build critter houses from simple materials that you can purchase at a home-improvement center. You may even be able to recycle materials you already have.

FAMILY PROJECT: INSTALLING A BAT BOX

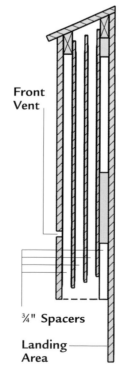

Front Vent

¾" Spacers

Landing Area

Well-designed bat boxes that are installed properly will attract some species of bat. Many bats need surprisingly warm temperatures inside a bat box (anywhere from 85 to 100 degrees), so mount yours in an area that receives a lot of sun. In northern areas, stain your bat box dark brown to help it retain heat. Attach the box 15 or 20 feet off the ground. In order to fly, bats jump from a perch, drop, and then spread their wings. If your bat box is mounted too low, bats won't have the space they need to drop and take flight and therefore won't move in. Attach bat boxes to the side of the house or on poles. Those attached to trees give predators such as raccoons easy access.

COMMON BATS THAT USE BAT BOXES

These bat species commonly use properly mounted bat boxes as a source of cover.

- Little brown bat
- Big brown bat
- Mexican free-tailed bat
- Pallid bat
- Long-eared myotis
- Southeastern bat

▶ Little brown bat

ADDING BAT BOXES

There are more species of bats in the world than any other group of mammal. They play a key role in the ecosystem by consuming millions of insects every night, some of which are human pests. Not all bats eat insects, however. Amazingly, some bats eat nectar, fish, frogs, birds, small mammals, and even blood from large mammals and birds (There are three species of vampire bats, all native to Mexico or to Central and South America.) Contrary to myth, bats don't get caught in people's hair, and they don't suck human blood. Each bat species has its own cover requirements. Some roost in caves, but many others find cover in tree cavities or even under loose pieces of bark. A few bat species will also use boxes as places to raise their young. Bat boxes can replace valuable bat habitat that has been lost.

THE TRUTH ABOUT BUTTERFLY HOUSES

Not all popular critter houses actually benefit wildlife. Butterfly houses can add a nice decorative touch to a garden design, but butterflies rarely, if ever, use them. Butterflies prefer natural cover in dense vegetation or human-made cover like brush piles to fill their need for cover, so keep this in mind before buying a butterfly house.

▲ Although ornamental, butterfly houses rarely attract butterflies, which prefer natural cover.

▲ An old clay flowerpot placed upside down in the shade makes a welcoming "toad abode."

AMPHIBIAN HOUSES

You can also make a critter house designed for the special needs of amphibians such as frog, toads, and salamanders. Again, you have the option of purchasing a decorative "toad abode" or making one on your own by recycling an old clay flowerpot. Simply use a hammer to crack off a small section of the lip of the pot; then place it in a shady part of your yard, upside down. The clay pot will help retain humidity and provide a cool, dark place for toads, frogs, and other moisture-loving amphibians to find cover from the drying sun and from predators as well. Add a shallow water dish to make the house more attractive to these amphibians. The drainage dish of the clay pot or even an old pie pan will work perfectly.

LEARNING TO LOVE TOADS

Toads are wonderfully lumpy and bumpy wildlife species that should be welcomed into your Backyard Wildlife Habitat garden or landscape. Toads are really just a specific group of frogs, generally characterized by dry, bumpy skin, stubby legs, blunt snouts, and a preference for walking rather than hopping. These adaptations allow toads to be more terrestrial than other frogs, and many toads spend time in the water only for mating, preferring to burrow into the ground for cover. Toad "warts" are not warts at all. They are actually glands that produce foul-tasting secretions that deter predators. Toads have great value for any wildlife landscape. They, like most amphibians, will eat anything that moves and is small enough to fit in their mouths. They relish slugs and insect pests and, for this reason, make excellent garden inhabitants.

▲ Toads (left) are more stocky and terrestrial than their frog cousins (right).

FAMILY PROJECT: AMBHIBIAN HOUSE

In addition to a toad abode, you can create a house that will be used by terrestrial frogs, toads, and salamanders. Most amphibians have sensitive skin and need to find moist, dark cover from the sun. You can accomplish this using some scrap plywood and material you find around your yard. Just be sure to select a shady spot that is surrounded by cover. You can also include additional cover in your overall design.

1 *Select a piece of scrap plywood or untreated lumber. The larger the piece of plywood, the more cover will be provided by your amphibian house. Select a shady spot near water; dig a 2-inch-deep depression that is the same dimension as your piece of plywood. Place several fist-sized rocks in the corners of one side of the depression as shown in the illustration. The tops of the rocks should stick out over the top of the depression by at least 1 inch.*

2 *Lay the piece of plywood over the depression. One end should lie flat on the ground in the depression. The other end should be propped up on either side by the rocks, creating an entry point for amphibians and other wildlife.*

3 *Cover the plywood with several inches of mulch or old leaves, and plant native wildflowers or shrubs around the perimeter for added cover. For a multilayer cover feature, build a brush pile on top of the amphibian house. Place a water dish nearby.*

chapter five

Providing Places to Raise Young

All wildlife species need places to bear and raise their young. This is a habitat component that includes space to engage in courtship and mating, space and materials for nest building, space to dig dens and burrows, safe conditions for egg laying or live birth, and adequate resources for both juveniles and for adults. You can help make a difference for wildlife populations in your region by providing this important habitat component.

◀ Installing and maintaining nesting boxes can support bird populations in your area.

NATURAL NESTING PLACES

In the same way that native plant communities provide the best sources of food and cover for wildlife, they also provide a diverse array of wildlife with the resources necessary for raising their young. For example, woodlands and grasslands are native plant communities that provide important nesting places as well as the cover needed by young wildlife. These areas also provide the the raw materials that many species of birds, insects, and mammals need to build nests or line birthing dens.

Exotic plants can have a negative impact on the ability of

wildlife to raise their young. One six-year study of an area near Chicago found that invasive exotic shrubs such as Amur honeysuckle (*Lonicera maackii*) and European buckthorn (*Rhamnus cathartica*) have given predators easier access to American robin and wood thrush nests than do the locally native shrubs and trees traditionally used by these birds, including viburnum (*Viburnum* spp.), hawthorn (*Crataegus* spp.), maple (*Acer* spp.), and rough-barked hop hornbeam (*Ostrya* spp.).

NESTING IN SNAGS

In addition to providing much-needed cover, both snags (standing dead trees) and woody debris provide important places for many wildlife species to raise their young. Insects burrow into the wood and form nests or egg chambers. Many insect species spend their larval phase in dead wood and become important food sources for creatures higher on the food chain. Many cavity-nesting birds and mammals use holes in snags as nesting areas. Woodpeckers actually excavate cavities in declining trees and snags, and the cavities are then used by many other cavity nesters.

Some species bear their young or lay their eggs underneath fallen logs and other large woody debris. Unbelievably, black bear females often spend their winter dormancy high up inside partially hollowed trees. During this dormancy, bears give birth to tiny, helpless cubs that grow so rapidly on their mother's rich milk that they are capable of keeping up with their mother and foraging by the time spring approaches and they leave the den.

Many birds and mammals will also nest or den inside a brush pile. Others will use the smaller twigs and branches from a brush pile as a source of materials for nest building.

▲ An American robin feeds her young.

▲ American cranberry viburnum (*Vibumum trilobum*) is a nesting shrub for robins and wood thrushes.

◄ This lush backyard habitat is located in St. John's, MI.

NESTING PLACES YOU PROVIDE

Restoring native plant communities and other natural landscape features will provide places to raise young for a diverse collection of native wildlife. You can also install features to provide this important habitat component for specific groups of wildlife. The rest of this chapter will cover specific places to raise young for some of the most popular groups of wildlife that will utilize your habitat.

BIRD NESTING AREAS

Many bird species construct nests, where they lay their eggs and raise their young. Some birds nest on the ground or in the branches of trees. Many others build nests in tree holes. Nesting boxes replicate these natural nesting cavities.

Not all nesting cavities are created equal in the eyes of different bird species. Each species has specific requirements, ranging from hole size to depth of cavity. Your nesting box must meet these requirements for the species you wish to use it to move in. Once birds discover your nesting boxes, your yard will become a flurry of activity as the birds begin nest building and feeding their young.

◄ A black-capped chickadee enters a backyard nesting box.

◄ A nesting box is outfitted with a predator guard.

▼ An American robin is shown incubating on nest platform.

FAMILY PROJECT: BIRD NESTING BOXES

Installing a nesting box is a fun project that will provide you with hours of wildlife viewing opportunities. Nesting boxes must be installed properly in order to provide a safe place for birds to bear and raise their young. Backyard birding specialists at Wild Birds Unlimited® recommend the following nesting box tips:

- Select a nesting box for functional purposes rather than decorative ones. Decorative boxes often lack the specific features that are attractive to birds.
- The entry hole must be the right size for the species you are trying to attract.
- The box dimensions and the distance from the entry hole to the floor of the box must be appropriate to accommodate different species' needs.
- The wood used should be at least ¾ inch thick to provide insulation for the nest.
- Natural, untreated wood is best. You can stain the wood using a nontoxic product, but do not paint it. Dark stains will absorb sunlight, which could cause excessive heat in the box.
- There should be an operative panel for monitoring and cleaning the box.
- The box should have ventilation holes drilled in the upper portion of the sides and drainage holes in the bottom.
- A sloping roof will allow water to run off and help keep the nest dry.
- Score the walls of the interior of the box to help baby birds leave the nest when they are ready to fledge.
- The box should not have a perch. Perches allow predators and exotic birds access to the nest. Special guards can be added to the entry hole and mounting pole to keep predators and exotics out.
- Cornell University's Lab of Ornithology is the recognized authority on nesting boxes for birds. Contact the Cornell Birdhouse Network project online at http://birds.cornell.edu.

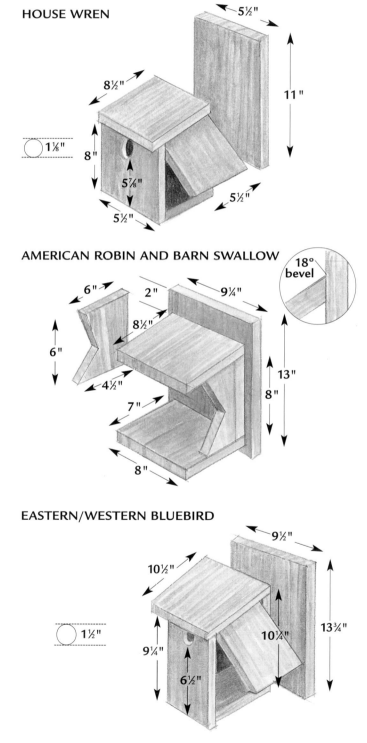

HOUSE WREN

AMERICAN ROBIN AND BARN SWALLOW

EASTERN/WESTERN BLUEBIRD

▲ A female eastern bluebird is seen feeding a fledgling. Pesticides deprive birds of a valuable food source.

HELP WITH NESTS

You can help birds find nesting material by building a brush pile, planting a meadow, or placing pet hair and small bits of thread outside. Birds will use these materials to build their nests. Avoid cottons, which retain moisture and can make the nest too damp.

If you're deciding whether or not to use pesticides, remember to factor in the effect these chemicals will have on bird populations. Insects are the primary food source for baby birds. Without healthy insect populations, parent birds cannot feed their young. Many pesticides can harm or kill the birds themselves as well.

Just as important as protecting birds and their food sources from pesticides is monitoring your nesting boxes for invasive exotic species. Aggressive exotics such as European starlings and English sparrows can drive out native bird species, such as bluebirds. Learn to identify these exotic species and their nests. If you discover exotic species in your nesting boxes, you should remove their nests to discourage egg laying.

DEALING WITH BABY BIRDS

Down-covered baby birds that have not left the nest are called nestlings. Once their flight feathers develop, young birds leap from the nest for their first flight and are then called fledglings. However, most birds cannot master the ability to fly immediately. Some spend as long as two weeks in this fledgling stage. During this period, they hop around on the ground or in low vegetation exercising their wings and learning to fly. Their parents continue to feed them throughout this fledgling period.

If you find a down-covered nestling on the ground, the best thing to do is to locate the nest and return the baby to it. The adult won't reject the baby because of human scent—in fact, most birds have poor sense of smell and won't even perceive human odor. If you can't locate or reach the nest, contact a licensed wildlife rehabilitator to provide care for the bird. (Call a local nature center or county animal control agency to be put in contact with a rehabilitator.) If you find a feathered fledgling on the ground, leave it alone. Many fledglings are picked up by well-meaning people who think they've been abandoned. While this is a vulnerable time for young birds and some fall prey to natural predators, it is part of the natural food chain. Raising baby birds by hand is unnatural and is very difficult. It should be left to licensed wildlife rehabilitators.

While many nestlings and fledglings become food for natural predators in the food chain, many others become victims of free-roaming domestic cats. This unnatural predation can affect bird populations and deprive native predators of important food sources. If you have a pet cat, protect the birds—and your cat—by keeping it indoors.

▲ A northern cardinal provides insects to nestlings.

▲ Take care not to disturb nests you find on your property. Shown is a gray catbird nest with eggs.

87

PROJECT: BEE NESTING HOUSES

You can create a nesting place that will be used by a variety of native bees. Orchard mason bees (*Osmia lignaria* and related species), which are important pollinators of both native plants and agricultural crops, will be attracted to and use bee nesting houses. At least a dozen species of these bees can be found in each state and Canadian province. Bees will use the tunnels in these nesting houses to lay a series of eggs, each of which is supplied with a pollen ball to serve as a food source for the hatchling.

Place the bee house on the south side of the building, fence post, or tree so that the house receives sun for most of the day. Once you've placed a bee house, do not attempt to move it until November when nesting activity as ceased.

▶ The over 4,000 species of bees are North America's most important pollinators.

▶ A hummingbird moth feeds on verbena (*Verbena bonareinsis*).

▼ Anna's hummingbird is shown pollinating autumn sage (*Salvia gregii*).

1 Cut 8 to 10 bamboo stalks into 5 inch pieces. Using a screwdriver, hollow out 3½ inches from one end.

2 Tie the bamboo in a bundle and hang it in a sunny spot.

An alternative is to drill a number of ⁵⁄₁₆-inch holes in untreated scrap lumber. Drill 3 to 5 inches deep but not all the way through the wood.

You can cover the holes with chicken wire to help keep birds away from the bee house.

POLLINATORS

Pollinators are a diverse group of wildlife species that fertilize plants while moving from flower to flower in search of nectar, pollen, or nesting materials. Once fertilized, plant blossoms form berries, fruits, vegetables, and seed heads, which are critical food sources in natural food chains as well as for people. These pollination services are critical to the health of ecosystems. Most pollinator species are also easily provided for in habitat gardens. The primary groups of wildlife responsible for pollination are bees, butterflies, moths, flies, beetles, hummingbirds, and some species of bats.

Bees are our most effective and important pollinators. In North America alone, there are over 4,000 species of native bees. Most of these do not form hives and are nonaggressive. Most rarely, if ever, sting. Often, it's not the availability of flowers and nectar that limits bee populations in an area but rather the availability of appropriate nesting sites.

▲ A variegated fritillary caterpillar (top) is feeding on passion vine (*Passiflora incarnata*). The butterfly of the species is shown above.

OTHER POLLINATORS

Butterflies and moths are also important pollinators, and both require specific resources, called host plants, for their caterpillars to grow. Butterflies and moths have evolved very closely with the native plants of their region, and most rely solely on a small group of plants as food sources for their young. In some cases, the butterfly or moth caterpillar can eat only one type of plant. Without the appropriate host plant for these pollinators, you will not be providing a complete habitat for these lovely insects.

Adult hummingbirds feed primarily on nectar found in long, tube-shaped flowers. However, hummingbirds cannot survive on nectar alone. Insects form a significant portion of a hummingbird's diet and are the only food source for nestlings. Without healthy insect populations, hummingbirds cannot feed their young, and these important pollinators will not be sustained in your area.

Pesticides pose a significant threat to many pollinator species and their young. Both adult and larval bees, flies, butterflies, moths, and beetles will all be killed by insecticides. The caterpillars of native butterfly and moth species do little or no long-term damage to their host plants. Consider the beauty of the winged adults when you see caterpillar nibble marks on the plants in your landscape. If you spray the caterpillars, you won't be able to enjoy the beauty of the adult insects. Similarly, if you use pesticides on the insects in your garden or landscape, hummingbirds will not be able to find the insects needed to feed their young.

◄ A monarch caterpillar (far left) is about to transition to pupa. An adult monarch (left) lands on swamp milkweed (*Asclepias incarnata*).

PROJECT: PLANT A BUTTERFLY GARDEN

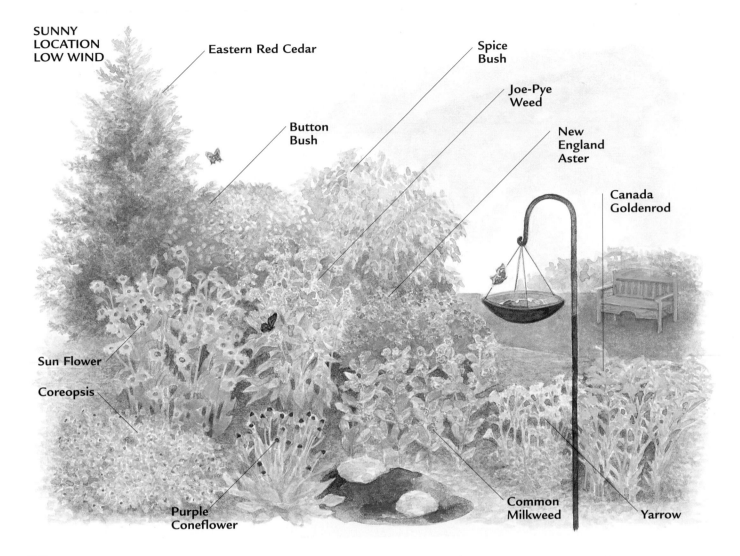

SUNNY LOCATION LOW WIND

Eastern Red Cedar

Spice Bush

Joe-Pye Weed

Button Bush

New England Aster

Canada Goldenrod

Sun Flower

Coreopsis

Purple Coneflower

Common Milkweed

Yarrow

You can provide for adult butterflies simply by planting a garden full of nectar-providing plants. If you want a true butterfly garden, however, you'll need to provide for caterpillars as well.

▪ Select a sunny location that you can easily see from your house, deck, patio, or other viewing area.

▪ Provide cover nearby with shrubs or perhaps a brush pile. A densely planted shrub row will also act as a wind-break—gardens in windy locations are less attractive to butterflies.

▪ Provide a shallow water source or puddling area. (See "Puddles and Muddy Areas," page 57.)

▪ Plant native shrubs and wildflowers that provide nectar. Butterflies prefer species that have flat flower heads, such as asters, coreopsis, and yarrow, on which they can land and sip nectar with their straw-like proboscis. Plants with white or pale colored flowers and strong musky scent, such as yucca and moonflower, will attract night-flying moths.

▪ Plant host plants for caterpillars. (See "Host Plants for Butterflies," page 98.)

▪ Never use pesticides in or near your butterfly garden.

▪ You can also add a butterfly nectar feeder or a feeder that holds rotting fruit. (See "Butterfly Feeders," page 43.)

YOUNG HERPTILES

When spoken of collectively, reptiles and amphibians are called herptiles, or herps for short. Most herptiles lay eggs, but some give live birth. Reptile eggs have leathery shells and are deposited on land. Amphibian eggs are soft and must be kept moist or submerged in clean water. Keep this in mind as you plan places for these groups of wildlife to raise young.

Reptiles such as snakes, lizards, and turtles typically lay their eggs in nests dug in the ground formed in a sheltered spot beneath rocks, woody debris, or mulch piles, or in dense vegetation. While most amphibians lay their eggs in water, some salamanders lay their eggs in very moist areas on land underneath rocks and woody debris. All these places will also provide young herptiles with cover.

Amphibians such as frogs, toads, and salamanders lay their soft, moist eggs in jelly-like masses or long strings. Because they are moist, amphibian eggs must be laid in standing bodies of clean water. If they dry out, the embryos inside the eggs will die. Water features designed for amphibian breeding should be well planted with native aquatic and wetland plants. These plants will provide cover for tadpoles and salamander larvae. Many amphibian species lay their eggs in temporary ponds called vernal pools that dry up in the summer or dry season. Because of this, vernal pools can't support fish, which are major predators of amphibian larvae. Without smaller, fishless ponds, many amphibians cannot survive in your yard or neighborhood. Wildlife-oriented water features should also be free of ornamental fish like koi and goldfish, which will consume the eggs and young of aquatic amphibians.

▼ A five-lined skink guards eggs at its nest. Many reptiles dig nests for egg laying.

A DIFFERENT TYPE OF PARENTING

Herptile eggs and young are important food sources for many predators. To ensure the survival to adulthood of at least some individuals, most have developed a reproduction strategy that produces many young. Unlike most birds, which usually lay no more than three or four eggs in a nest, some turtles can lay up to 30 or 40 eggs, and frogs can lay hundreds of individual eggs.

Also unlike most mammals and birds, most herps provide little, if any, care for their young. While this results in higher individual mortality of eggs and young, the sheer number of eggs laid and babies born ensures that some will survive to adulthood and the population will continue. However, be sure to provide adequate natural cover for young herps—both on land and in the water—because they receive no parental protection from predators. Free-roaming domestic cats take an unnatural toll on both adult and juvenile herps, as they do on birds. For this reason, cats should be kept indoors.

Reptiles emerge from the egg as miniature versions of adults and have the same food, water, and cover requirements as adults. Since most amphibians have an aquatic phase when they breathe through gills, they require habitat similar to that for young fish: clean water with plenty of vegetation for cover. Amphibians later metamorphose into adults and develop lungs. Once metamorphosis is complete, the juveniles have the same habitat needs as fully grown adult individuals.

All herptiles are ectotherms, which means that they do not produce their own heat as mammals and birds do but rather are dependent on the outside environment for their temperature regulation. Reptiles need to bask in the sun to help raise their body temperatures. This also helps them absorb important vitamins and is critical to the growth of young animals into healthy adults. Because they cannot regulate their temperatures internally, herps that live in areas with excessively cold seasons must hibernate to survive. Some species bury themselves in the ground under layers of dead leaves and woody debris or in natural caves and crevices. Others hibernate in the mud and leaves at the bottom of ponds and lakes.

▲ Water features provide needed cover.

▼ A hatchling turtle needs cover from predators.

chapter six

Designing Your Wildlife Habitat

Gardens by their very nature are works of art designed to welcome people. Your challenge is to create a garden that meets the needs of wildlife by restoring natural habitat but still draws you and your family, neighbors, and friends into it. Look to natural wilderness for design inspiration. Keep this guiding principle in mind when you design your Backyard Wildlife Habitat plan.

◄ Look to nature for inspiration in designing your backyard habitat.

ASSESSING YOUR PROPERTY

Begin by assessing your current landscape to determine what you already have and its condition. Use the following lists as guides. You'll find it helpful to actually write down the answers to these questions.

- What plant species do you already have?
- What plant communities are represented?
- Which of your plants are native? Exotic? Invasive?
- Are any plantings overgrown or out of place?
- What percentage of the property is lawn?
- How much lawn do you and your family actually use?
- What types of soils occur on your property?
- What is the direction of the prominent wind?
- What is the sun exposure for each part of the property?
- What microclimates exist on the property?
- What is the topography of the property? Which areas are low and retain water, and which areas are higher and drier?
- What is the location of any underground power lines?
- Are there any entry points where wildlife might gain access to your house that need repair?
- How will your neighbors take to a naturalistic landscape?

▼ Decide which species you want to attract to your backyard habitat.

▶ Survey the conditions of your yard and make a wish list of the native plants you want to include.

Create a wish list for your Backyard Wildlife Habitat garden.

- What percentage of the property do you want to devote to wildlife gardening and how much needs to be kept mown or open for human use?
- What kinds of wildlife do you want to attract?
- What is your budget?
- What colors would you like to see in the garden?
- What"hardscape" features, such as patios, retaining walls, gazebos, or other structures, would you like?
- Do you need play areas for children?
- Do you or your neighbors have outdoor dogs or cats?
- Are there any special viewing points that you'd like to preserve or create?
- What are the top priorities for this season? Next season?

NATIVE PLANT GUIDE

The National Wildlife Federation and its eNature Web site have partnered with the Lady Bird Johnson Wildflower Center to create a searchable online database that provides color photos and detailed descriptions of many of the most popular native plants. You can get access to the Native Plant Guide at http://www.nwf.org/backyardwildlife-habitat/.

PURCHASING NATIVE PLANTS

Unlike conventional gardens, an ideal wildlife garden will contain as many native plant species as possible. Native plants are the foundation of habitat in the wild and should be part of your Backyard Wildlife Habitat garden.

Although some native species have been garden center staples for years, finding a great variety of natives at your local retail garden or home center can be challenging. The horticulture and landscaping industries are just beginning to recognize the ecological and economic value of working with native plants. Some companies label native species to make it easier for native plant enthusiasts to find the appropriate plants.

Many nurseries that sell native plants often offer only specially bred or cloned hybrids or cultivars that have been chosen for their landscape value. A variety is a specific type of a species. Varieties occur naturally or are created by people through selective breeding. A cultivar (short for cultivated variety) is a variety that has been created by breeding or cloning. A hybrid is a cross between two species. Unfortunately, selective breeding for ornamental qualities often affects the qualities that made the plant beneficial to wildlife, and cloning can result in a loss of the genetic diversity that occurs naturally in the wild.

HOST PLANTS FOR BUTTERFLIES

BUTTERFLY SPECIES	CATERPILLAR HOST PLANT
◼ Monarch	Milkweed (*Asclepias* spp.)*
◼ Tiger Swallowtail	Willow (*Salix* spp.)
◼ Mourning Cloak	Elm (*Ulmus* spp.)
◼ Gulf Fritillary	Passionflower* (*Passiflora* spp.)
◼ Question Mark	Hackberry (*Celtis* spp.)
◼ Buckeye	Plantain (*Plantago* spp.)
◼ Wood Nymph	Purple-top grass (*Tridens flavus*)

**These species rely exclusively on these host plants.*

▲ Question mark butterfly

IDENTIFYING PLANTS

You can identify which plants are cultivars by looking at the names on their plant tags or plant descriptions. Every plant has a common name and a scientific name. The common name of a plant is written first, followed by the italicized scientific name in parenthesis. An example of this is river birch (*Betula nigra*). Cultivars are given special names by their breeders or cloners. These special names are listed in quotation marks on the plant tag after the common and scientific names. A popular cultivar of river birch is 'Heritage'. The plant tag for this cultivar would read River Birch (*Betula nigra* 'Heritage'). Hybrids are indicated by an "x" in the scientific name. An example of this is the hybrid cultivar of two shrubs, fragrant sage (*Salvia clevelandii*) and purple sage (*Salvia leucophylla*), both western natives. The hybrid name is gray musk sage (*Salvia x clevelandii* 'Pozo Blue').

Reading plant tags will give you important information that will help you make your plant selections. Cultivars and hybrids of natives aren't necessarily bad choices for wildlife, and often they are the only options available through retail garden centers. Think of cultivars and hybrids as domesticated versions of wild plants. Releasing packs of domestic dogs into the wild isn't the same thing as restoring gray wolf populations, even though all dogs are descended from wolves and they are genetically similar enough to inter-breed. Sticking to the original native plant species when you can is the best plan if you're working to restore a functioning bit of the ecosystem.

▶ This clematis is a hybrid as indicated by its scientific name (*clematis x jackmanii*).

▼ Plant tags can help you choose plants. Below is yellow jasmine (*Gelsemium sempervirens*).

▲ Select plants for their wildlife value. Even when space is limited, such as it is in this yard, there is still plenty of room to create wildlife habitat.

LEARN ABOUT LOCAL CONDITIONS

To locate nurseries that sell plants that are wild native species to your area, learn about the plants that currently grow in your yard and neighborhood. You'll be surprised to find that many of the plants used in landscapes are not a part of the local ecosystem. Instead they come from other parts of the world and were chosen because of their functionality for human purposes. Ability to grow in poor soils, to withstand air pollution, to provide ornamental blooms and foliage, and to resist disease are plant characteristics that typically outweigh a plant's value to wildlife when people choose plants for their gardens. Even in seemingly natural rural areas, many common species are really exotics that have been introduced in the last century. The fact that we are used to seeing them and may mistake them for natural parts of the ecosystem does not change their negative impact on native plant and wildlife species.

LEARN ABOUT NATIVE PLANTS

There are many ways to learn which plant species are native. Field guides are a good place to start, but they typically describe the species that you might commonly see in a particular region, regardless of their true ecological origin. Local or state native plant societies provide more reliable information. They are dedicated to preserving and restoring the natural floral heritage of their region. Most have excellent native plant lists that can be obtained free of charge. Many also keep lists of nurseries that offer the appropriate native species for their region. Native plant society members themselves are often a wonderful source of native plants. Many members participate in plant swaps and sales using plants grown in their own gardens.

HOW NATIVE PLANTS ARE SOLD

Native plants are sold in a variety of different ways.

SEED

Herbaceous grasses and wildflowers are generally sold as seed, although some woody species are available as seed. Work with a nursery that specializes in native seeds for your area. Don't purchase seed mixes in a can as they often contain invasive exotic species.

PLUG

Plugs are seedlings of both herbaceous and woody plants that are usually one or two years old. Plugs are usually grown in narrow containers and sold with a small, dense rootball. Because plugs are small and relatively inexpensive, they are also a good choice for covering large areas.

WHIP

Whips are the cut branches of willow, poplar, and other woody species that will root from branch cuttings. Whips can be planted upright directly into the soil or placed horizontally in a shallow trench and then covered with soil. Whips are often used on slopes to control erosion of wetland areas. They are also relatively inexpensive.

BARE-ROOT

Both herbaceous and woody plant species are sold bare-root, which means all soil or other growing medium has been washed away from the rootball. Bare-root plants are typically sold via mail-order while dormant, and they are relatively inexpensive.

CONTAINERIZED OR POTTED

Both herbaceous and woody plants are sold in containers or pots, typically by retailers. Like the balled-and-burlapped stock, containerized plants are usually too heavy for shipping and require significant care in the retail nursery setting, and therefore are more expensive.

BALLED-AND-BURLAPPED

Large woody plants are typically sold in a retail nursery setting with their rootballs, complete with soil, wrapped in burlap. The plant's weight, size, and necessary care by a retail nursery (its overhead costs) increase the cost of balled-and-burlapped (often abbreviated as "B and B") stock and make mail-order sales prohibitively difficult and expensive. But B-and-B stock will have an instant effect on the landscape.

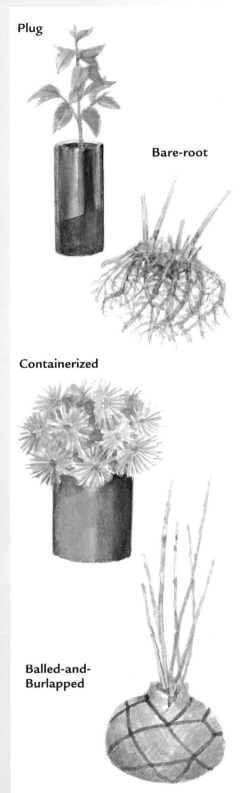

Plug

Bare-root

Containerized

Balled-and-Burlapped

habitat hints: FINDING NATIVE PLANTS

- Contact your local native plant society to learn what plants are native to your region and which are invasives or other problematic exotics.
- Learn how to propagate plants from seeds and cuttings, and grow your own native plants.
- Participate in plant swaps with other native plant growers.
- Organize a plant rescue at a construction site.
- Let your local nursery know you will purchase native plants for wildlife if they are available and clearly marked as native.

Your native plant society will most likely provide you with information on mail-order nurseries. They are often the best source of affordable native plants for your garden. In fact, there is a whole network of mail-order nurseries that specialize in native plants.

These nurseries typically offer their plants through catalogs or via the Internet. The beauty of this type of plant shopping is that you have a greater variety of plant species and seeds from which to choose in comparison with the limited selection available at most garden centers. Plants are often sold bare-root, which means that all the soil has been washed away from their roots. Not only does this make them lighter for shipping, but it often reduces the cost of the plants because it's cheaper for the nursery to grow them in beds instead of containers.

PARTICIPATING IN PLANT RESCUES

Organized "plant rescues" provide another great way to get plants that are native to your area. Native plant societies or other

◀ Ruby-throated hummingbirds love the nectar they find in trumpet creeper (*Campsis radicans*). However, the plant may require regular maintenance when planted in a small garden.

conservation organizations often conduct the rescues, which take place in areas slated for development with the permission of the property owner. Not only does this save locally native plants from certain destruction, it is a free source of plant material for your garden.

Never collect plants from the wild unless you are participating in an authorized plant rescue. Many species have been pushed to the brink of extinction as a result of overenthusiastic plant collectors digging from the wild. Don't patronize nurseries that dig their plants from the wild. Ask to make sure that the plants for sale were both propagated and grown in the nursery. Be specific. A plant that was dug in the wild and then grown in a pot for a year might be labeled as "nursery grown."

AGGRESSIVE NATIVE PLANTS

As you select plants, keep in mind that some native plants are aggressive and are not the best choices for a small garden because they may dominate other plants. The difference between an aggressive native and an invasive exotic is that an aggressive native is kept in check in the wild and is part of a greater native plant community, while invasives dominate and take over entire native communities. Often, aggressive natives are pioneer species that are able to colonize disturbed areas and grow in poor soils. As they spread, their roots loosen the soil and their fallen leaves improve the soil. Other more particular native plants are then able to move in and eventually take over, and plant succession takes place. Invasive plants prevent other species from taking hold. Interestingly, aggressive natives often become invasive when planted outside their normal range.

Trumpet creeper (*Campsis radicans*) is an example of an aggressive native plant. It is beautiful and a favorite of ruby-throated hummingbirds and insects, but it requires regular maintenance to keep it under control in small spaces.

In any region, you'll find a great variety of native plant species that can meet your landscaping needs and are suited to almost every condition. Be sure to tell the local garden center or nursery that you'd like them to carry and label native plant species.

▲▼ Some natives are aggressive spreaders, so they can colonize new areas. Shown above is Eastern red cedar (*Juniperus virginiana*); shown below is smooth sumac (*Rhus glabra*). Both help enrich the soil for other species.

GARDEN DESIGN APPROACHES

Once you've assessed your property, gained a sense of the site-specific conditions, and done some research on native plant resources for your area, you're ready to start planting. The design of the garden or landscape is just as important as the plants you select. Conventional planting approaches offer limited habitat for wildlife. Here are some alternative planting approaches that will help you design your habitat.

▲ Planting for wildlife differs from planting a conventional garden.

BUILDING WITHIN THE ENVELOPE

If you are building a new house on an undeveloped lot, survey the plant communities that already exist there. If one portion of the property has a healthy plant community, consider preserving that area and locate the house, if possible, in an area with invasive exotics or less-established plants. Save the trees that provide the best value to local wildlife. (Remember that fallen or dying trees provide a lot of wildlife habitat.)

▲ Habitat can develop quickly. Here is a water feature at installation (left), after one month (middle), and after one year (right).

Once you've identified the plants that you want to save, work with the contractor to protect the vegetation from damage during construction. Mark these areas with white construction ribbon (available at most hardware stores or home centers).

Protect the root zones of individual trees by blocking off the area to prevent heavy equipment from compacting the roots. To determine how far the underground roots extend, multiply the diameter of the tree trunk by 1.2.

The end result should be an "envelope" of vegetation around the site of the new house that is clearly marked off and safe from damage by machinery. The contractor and his machinery will then operate entirely within this envelope during construction, and you will have a beautiful, established habitat when you move into your new house.

STARTING FROM SCRATCH

If you have recently moved into a newly built house, you may find yourself the proud owner of a piece of land that has been scraped clean of every bit of vegetation as well as the original topsoil. You will be starting with a blank canvas on which you can build your wildlife garden. The entire property may be seeded with lawn grass. Begin defining beds and other habitat features as soon as possible, before your lawn is established.

Resist the urge to buy prepackaged "wildflower" seed mixes, because they may contain invasive exotic species.

NATIVE GRASSES AND SEDGES

These are just a few of the many native grasses and sedges that provide wildlife with food, cover, and nesting material. Some are best planted in natural prairie or meadow patches along with wildflowers, but some can actually be grown and maintained as lawn—without all of the watering, fertilizing, and mowing, of course. Check with your native plant society for a list of grasses native to your area.

- Baltimore sedge (*Carex senta*)
- Blue grama (*Buuteloua gracilis*)
- Blue wildrye (*Elymus glaucus*)
- Big bluestem (*Andropogon gerardii*)
- Bottlebrush grass (*Elymus hystrix*)
- Broomsedge (*Andropogon virginicus*)
- Buffalograss (*Buchloe dactyloides*)
- California meadow sedge (*Carex pansa*)
- Canada wild rye (*Elymus canadensis*)
- Catlin sedge (*Carex texensis*)
- Hairy-awn muhly (*Muhlenbergia capillaries*)
- Indiangrass (*Sorghastrum nutans*)
- Junegrass (*Koeleria macrantha*)
- Little bluestem (*Schizachyrium scoparium*)
- Pennsylvania sedge (*Carex pensylvanica*)
- Prairie cordgrass (*Spartina pectinata*)
- Prairie dropseed (*Sporobolus heterolepis*)
- Purple lovegrass (*Eragrostis spectabilis*)
- Red fescue (*Festuca rubra*)
- River oats/Northern sea oats (*Chasmanthium latifolium*)
- Saltgrass (*Distichlis spicata*)
- Sideoats grama (*Bouteloua curtipendula*)
- Sheep fescue (*Festuca ovina*)
- Switchgrass (*Panicum virgatum*)
- Texas hill country sedge (*Carex perdendtata*)
- Wiregrass (*Aristida stricta*)

REPLACING EXOTICS

In almost all cases, there is an analogous species native to your area that will support wildlife better than its exotic counterpart. Here's a good example:

SERVICEBERRY
FOR BRADFORD PEAR

Bradford pear (*Pyrus calleryana 'Bradford'*) is a ubiquitously planted cultivar of a tree native to China. Despite the fact that it is a weak tree prone to storm damage, its beautiful white flowers in spring and compact branching structure have made this tree a favorite for landscapes across the country. Bradford

(continued on page 108)

▲ Serviceberry (*Amelanchier* spp.) is a native replacement for the exotic Bradford pear (*Pyrus calleryana*).

THE WAIT-AND-SEE APPROACH

Allowing the plants you already have to grow freely and spread is another way of creating habitat. Rigidly pruned plants, when left to grow in a more natural, less contained way, will provide more cover for wildlife. Left to grow, a lawn or manicured garden will follow the natural process of succession, and other species will begin to colonize.

There are some downsides to this approach. Keep in mind that it may be difficult for the seeds of native plants to make their way into your garden naturally by wind or wildlife, especially if you live somewhere that doesn't have wild areas nearby to serve as seed sources. The seeds that do show up may be from invasive exotic species. The same wild look that will be attractive to wildlife may be decidedly unattractive to your neighbors. Be sure to talk with your neighbors and explain why you'd like to create a naturalistic landscape.

THE REMOVE-AND-REPLACE APPROACH

Remove plants that are invasive or have little value to wildlife, and replace them with native species that are appropriate for your site. In this way, you can slowly change a relatively sterile, conventional landscape into a more productive, native-based one. The benefit of this approach is that you can make as many or as few changes as your time and budget will allow within a given season. Another benefit is that this habitat style can mimic popular garden designs. For example, if your garden is planted in a formal style or your plantings follow a particular color scheme, you can keep the design and preserve the look you enjoy by replacing problematic exotic plants with similarly sized and colored native ones that are suited to the site.

THE BULL'S-EYE APPROACH

Another planting option for those who cannot have a completely wild landscape is the "bull's-eye" approach. Think of your house—the human habitat—as the center of a bull's eye surrounded by concentric planting rings. You can begin with the first planting ring, the one surrounding the house, by creating planting beds around the foundation. If you are going to feature ornamental exotics or cultivars (noninvasive, of course), or would like to showcase a neat and formal planting design, this is the best place to do it.

The second ring is the place for lawn. You'll want to keep in mind your specific use of lawn and determine how much you actually need and use, but surrounding your foundation planting with a bit of lawn will also help give your property an orderly appearance.

Beyond the foundation and lawn is where the real fun begins. Maybe you'll let the lawn transition into a meadow or prairie patch. Or you can let the lawn blend into a wetland area, per-

CONSERVE WATER

Native plants thrive under natural precipitation levels and usually don't require supplemental watering. If you must water, use drip irrigation or a soaker hose rather than a sprinkler. These methods apply water directly to the root zone of the plants, which reduces water loss due to evaporation.

BULL'S-EYE LANDSCAPE DESIGN

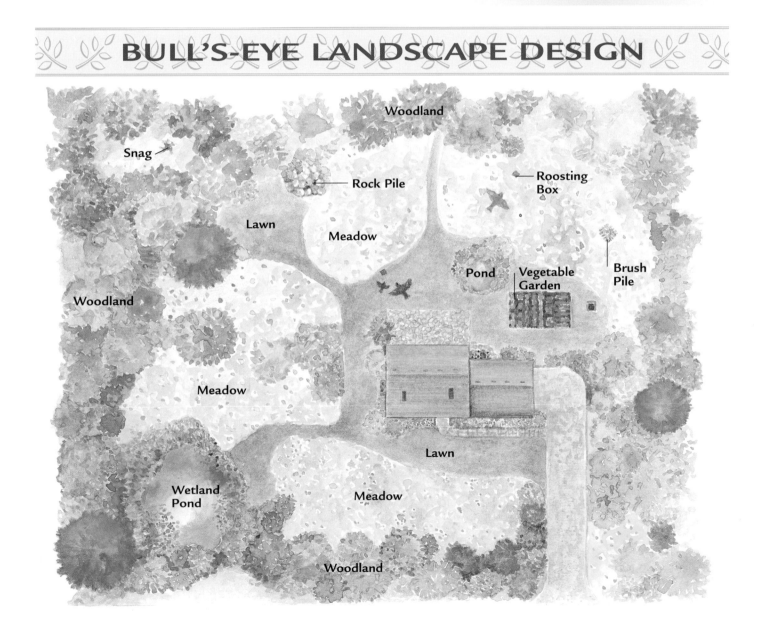

REPLACING EXOTICS

(continued from page 106)
pear, however, has little wildlife value other than to support exotic European starlings. It has also begun to hybridize and escape cultivation, and has been added to the invasive plant lists of several states.

A good native alternative to Bradford pear that will serve the same purpose in the landscape is serviceberry (*Amelanchier* spp.). Serviceberry is covered in beautiful white blossoms in the early spring and produces nutritious berries relished by many bird species, including waxwings, orioles, bluebirds, catbirds, and thrushes. In autumn, serviceberry leaves turn red, pink, or orange. Serviceberry is also commonly called juneberry, sarvis, or shadbush.

Collectively the following serviceberry species cover most of the United States and lower Canada:
- Allegheny serviceberry
  (*Amelanchier laevis*)
- Canadian serviceberry
  (*Amelanchier canadensis*)
- Downy serviceberry
  (*Amelanchier arborea*)
- Utah serviceberry
  (*Amelanchier utahensis*)
- Western serviceberry
  (*Amelanchier alnifolia*)

haps with a pond, where the yard naturally dips toward the back of the property. Behind the grassland or wetland area, you may want to plant a shrub row or a bramble patch, or allow the woody scrub to mix with the herbaceous grasses and wildflowers. If you live in an area where forests naturally occur, you can create and nurture a corner woodland pocket at the back, or even around the entire perimeter, of the property.

By using the bull's-eye approach, you can also take advantage of the edge effect. The edge effect refers to the greater diversity of wildlife that normally occurs where two different plant communities or ecosystems meet. A simplified example of the edge effect is the 35 species of songbirds that occur in an area where a meadow meets woodland. The meadow supports 15 species of birds adapted to open grassland; the woodland supports another 15 adapted specifically to dense tree cover; and the remaining five species are generalists that can live equally well in either plant community.

THE HOLISTIC APPROACH

The ultimate goal of creating a naturalistic, wildlife-friendly landscape is to restore a small piece of the natural ecosystem. The best way to accomplish this is to become an expert on the land upon which you live, learn its healthy and not-so-healthy aspects, and begin to coax it back into natural productivity and diversity. This holistic approach is very in-depth, but it will be the most rewarding for you and wildlife. Each of the previously described planting approaches can be incorporated into the holistic design method.

You can begin this process by doing some research and learning the natural history of the greater region that includes your property. Look to the natural areas around you for inspiration and to begin to learn what kind of native plant communities, in all stages of succession, occur in your area. Ask questions. What species of plants and animals existed where you now live 100 years ago? Do they still occur? If those species are no longer present in the landscape, why did they disappear? You'll want to learn the human history of the land as well, going all the way back to its first human inhabitants. How did your predecessors throughout history make a living from and affect the land? Which historical practices were sustainable, and which ones have led to environmental degradation? How many times has the natural vegetation been removed and regenerated? What exotic plants and animals have been introduced and become invasive? What are the natural soil types of the area, and in what condition is the soil now?

You can answer many of these questions by making a trip to your town hall. The planning and zoning commission should have historical information and sometimes even aerial photographs of your property and the surrounding land. The city or town's taxation department will have historical plat maps of your property and those that are adjacent to it. The local library, county extension service, native plant society, and historical society will all be helpful resources in your research as well.

Each question you ask will reveal clues about what you will need to do to restore habitat and the overall health of the land. You don't have to spend endless hours doing this research, but the information that you find will make you intimately familiar with the land upon which you currently live and will be invalu-

▲ Not all wildlife should live close to humans. For these species, fight to protect wilderness areas.

▲ Research the wildlife species native to your area.

▶ Develop a plan that allows you to create a section of wildlife habitat each season.

PROJECT: COMPOSTING 101

You can enrich your soil by recycling kitchen and yard waste by composting. You can purchase or build a compost bin, create a wire compost cage, or simply create a pile.

COMPOSTING TIPS

- Add a handful of garden soil to inoculate your pile with microorganisms that break down materials and create compost.
- Do not let the pile dry out. Keep it evenly moist but not wet.
- Turn the pile with a pitchfork to aerate it. Turning also speeds up the composting process.
- Compost is ready to be used in the garden when it is black and crumbly.

"GREEN" MATERIAL

These materials add nitrogen to compost:

- Grass clippings
- Tea bags
- Coffee grounds and filters
- Seaweed (available in coastal areas)
- Eggshells
- Fruit and vegetable scraps
- Nonwoody garden clippings
- Manure from grazing animals
  (cows, horses, goats, sheep)
- Manure and from small pets
  (rabbits, guinea pigs, hamsters)

"BROWN" MATERIAL

These materials add carbon to compost:

- Dead leaves/needles
- Sawdust from untreated wood
- Wood ashes
- Black and white newspaper
- Wood shavings or small pet bedding

UNACCEPTABLE MATERIAL

These materials can produce odors, attract pests, or spread weeds or disease and should not be composted:

- Meat
- Oils
- Weed seed heads
- Bones
- Dairy products
- Dog, cat, or other
  carnivorous pet waste

**COMPOST PILE
CROSS SECTION**

Coffee Grounds
Sawdust
Grass Clippings
Newspapers
Leaves

able to you as you plan your landscape.

As you explore the possibilities, consider the size of the space that you want to devote to habitat and the kinds of animals for which you'd like to provide. Your goal should be to provide a balanced ecosystem for a great variety of native wildlife. That doesn't mean you must provide for every species. Some wildlife cannot or should not live in close proximity to humans. Attracting large or predatory wildlife species, if they live in your area, can be dangerous for both people and wildlife. Fight to protect wilderness areas for those species, while doing what you can in your yard for species that can safely coexist with people.

Once you know the areas that need to be enhanced, you can begin selecting native plant species suited to the site. Most likely you won't be able to accomplish everything at once. It's alright to start small and take on one project at a time. You should enjoy habitat gardening year after year, making changes and improvements as you learn. By taking a holistic approach to habitat restoration, you can make even the smallest piece of land into a productive mini-ecosystem teeming with wildlife.

URBAN HABITATS

Whether the location is a balcony, a rooftop, an alley, or even a small city yard, urban habitat gardeners face a unique set of challenges. Many people believe that few species of wildlife will visit urban habitat gardens. On the contrary, providing habitat in urban areas can be even more important than providing it in suburban areas, where some resources for wildlife still exist. Urban wildlife species face the same daily rigors that their human counterparts face: lack of plants, little open space, trash, noise, and pollution. While it's true that not all wildlife species can tolerate urban conditions, a green urban oasis will be used and relished by a surprising array of city-living wildlife species.

The species that will be able to access your urban habitat area will be somewhat different from the species that will visit suburban and rural areas. Most large wildlife species won't make their way into urban centers. Neither will those species that

habitat hints:
FERTILIZE WITHOUT FERTILIZER

- Recycle yard "waste" like grass clippings, whole or shredded leaves, pine needles, chipped woody debris, or even old shredded newspaper by using it as mulch that will retain soil moisture, protect plant roots, and prevent erosion. Leave fallen leaves where they fall—this is nature's sustainable way of returning nutrients to the soil.

- Plant cover crops such as buckwheat and clover between plantings in your vegetable garden or seasonal flower beds to enrich the soil. Turn cover crops into the soil before planting because as they decompose they add more nutrients to the soil.

- Create a compost pile, and add kitchen scraps (no meats, fats, or bones) along with layers of nonwoody plant debris. An equal amount of "browns" like dead leaves and "greens" like grass clippings will provide a balance of nutrients.

- Start vermicomposting, or composting with worms. You can purchase worms and put them in a plastic bin with moistened newspaper. Add fruit and vegetable scraps, egg shells, and other kitchen waste, and soon you'll have compost enriched with nutrient-rich worm castings.

- Urge your community to start a municipal leaf composting program. The community will gain access to free or inexpensive compost for enriching individual and community gardens.

▲ Urban habitats, such as this one in Philadelphia, can attract a variety of wildlife.

▼ Create container gardens on balconies, patios, or rooftop gardens.

have very specific habitat requirements, like deep forests or open grassland—although you may be surprised at the adaptability of many species. Birds will definitely show up in a city habitat, and not just pigeons. A wide array of local and migratory songbirds and even raptors will visit urban gardens if food, water, and cover are present. They may even nest and lay eggs as well.

The next challenge faced by urban wildlife gardeners is the limited amount of available space for gardening. Another is poor quality or severely compacted urban soil, or even a complete lack of unpaved surfaces in which to plant. Additionally, many people living in urban areas rent their homes or apartments and do not want to invest in plants that they can't take with them if they move. Your options include container gardening and window boxes.

RURAL HABITATS

Rural properties offer opportunities for providing wildlife habitat that are different from urban or suburban properties. Rural areas already have higher wildlife populations and a greater diversity of species than do other areas with denser human populations. For this reason, people living in rural areas may not see the need to create and restore places for wildlife. The reality is that even rural areas have been affected by human encroachment, and in many places habitat has been degraded by new roads, new development, invasive exotic species, livestock and other domestic animals, waste runoff from factory farms, and heavy use of chemical pesticides and fertilizers.

Large tracts of land in rural areas often provide critical habitat for larger and potentially dangerous wildlife species. Learn which species may live on or use your property. It is important to learn how to provide for these species in a way that is safest for people as well as the wildlife. Species like black bears will be attracted to pet and livestock food that is improperly stored. Bird feeders may not be a good idea in areas with healthy bear populations. Living near wildlife like deer may also mean living near deer predators like mountain lions.

If allowed to roam free, domestic cats and dogs may become prey for wild predators. Be sure to keep your pets safely under your control at all times. Large hoofed animals like moose and elk can also be dangerous. Never try to touch or pet any wildlife species, no matter how cute or tame it looks. By keeping the unique circumstances—and opportunities—of owning and managing a large tract of rural land in mind, you will be able to safely view and appreciate these larger creatures.

BEST CONTAINER PLANTS

These common garden plants, some of which are North American natives, do well in containers and provide some element of habitat. Some provide hummingbirds and insects such as butterflies with nectar, while others are also host plants for butterfly caterpillars or produce seeds that will be eaten by birds.

- Clematis (*Clematis* spp.)
- Coreopsis (*Coreopsis* spp.)
- Dianthus (*Dianthus* spp.)
- Flowering tobacco (*Nicotiana* spp.)
- Lantana (*Lantana* spp.)
- Lavender (*Lavandula* spp.)
- Marigold (*Tagetes* spp.)
- Mint (*Mentha* spp.)
- Morning glory (*Ipomoea* spp.)
- Nasturtium (*Tropaeolum* spp.)
- Oregano (*Origanum* spp.)
- Parsley (*Petroselinum* spp.)
- Phlox (*Phlox* spp.)
- Rosemary (*Rosmarinus* spp.)
- Salvia (*Salvia* spp.)
- Sedum (*Sedum* spp.)
- Sunflower (*Helianthus* spp.)
- Verbena (*Verbena* spp.)
- Yarrow (*Achillea* spp.)
- Zinnia (*Zinnia* spp.)

◄ Even property in rural areas may need help when creating a wildlife habitat.

chapter seven

Human Dimensions of Habitat

Providing habitat for wildlife involves more than the science of ecology and wildlife populations. It is also about your connecting with nature where you live in a personal way. But beyond that, providing habitat is about creating the next generation of conservation stewards and spreading your knowledge to help others create habitat so that they too can experience nature in a personal way.

◄ Creating backyard habitats helps the whole family connect with nature.

YOUR PLACE IN THE LANDSCAPE

When providing wildlife habitat, remember to make a place for people as well. As you define your planting areas, look critically at your true usage of the landscape. Few people actually use their entire lawn area, for example. Perhaps you'd like an area of lawn for your annual family or church picnic, or for a play area for your children or grandchildren. Lawns can add definition to the more wild areas of your property, and they can provide viewpoints from your house or patio. Beyond those true uses of lawn, the rest of your property can be planted in a more natural fashion.

This doesn't mean that you won't ever visit the wilder parts of your property. On the contrary, you should be sure to plan space for people in your habitat areas, too. A wooden bench or mossy-green spot near a small pond or under a shade tree can be your own private haven to escape, unwind, relax, and observe the wonderful wildlife that live in your habitat.

You can create paths through natural areas by simply mowing a swath through a planted area or along its perimeter. Follow the curves of your garden beds or look to the natural topography of the land to give you an idea of where your path should be. You can use mulch or gravel to create paths as well.

HABITAT FOR KIDS

Children, too, will benefit from your habitat. They love secret spots in the garden where they can hide, think, get away from adults for a time, and connect with the natural world at their own pace. In today's modern society, children need outdoor experiences to introduce them to the natural wonders of the plants and animals that share their space. Allow the children in your life to assist in the creation of your habitat, and begin teaching them stewardship of the land at an early age.

habitat hints:

CHECKLIST FOR ENJOYING WILDLIFE

- ▣ Field guides
- ▣ Binoculars
- ▣ Notebook and pencil
- ▣ Magnifying lens
- ▣ Camera
- ▣ Comfortable viewing places

116

VOLUNTEER WITH NATIONAL WILDLIFE FEDERATION

The National Wildlife Federation has volunteer opportunities around the country that are designed to give you more in-depth training on wildlife, native plants, and habitat so that you can help others create and restore habitat. Habitat Stewards™ and Habitat Ambassadors™ opportunities provide additional training on providing habitat as well as the skills needed to teach others.

Call 800-822-9919 or go online at www.nwf.org/volunteer to learn about training opportunities in your area.

◀ Your backyard habitat plans should include areas where you can relax and enjoy the wildlife that visits your yard.

▶ The natural curiosity of kids will turn a visit to your wildlife habitat into a fun learning experinece.

FAMILY PROJECT: BUG HUNTING

Here is a great way for kids to learn about the tiny creatures that inhabit your Backyard Wildlife Habitat garden. Bury a clean metal can, such as a coffee can, so that the top of the can is even with ground level. Add a piece of fruit to the can. Place some stones around the opening, and lay a flat piece of wood over the stones. The opening should be just large enough to allow insects and other invertebrates to crawl into the

Stones

Cover

can. The smell of the fruit will attract them. Check the trap each day. Use a field guide or go to www.enature.com to identify and learn about the critters you've captured. For safety's sake, don't handle them, because some species can bite or sting. Don't keep the critters for more than a few hours, and always release them where you found them. The project is fun for adults, too.

Adapted from Ranger Rick® Magazine.

SHARE YOUR KNOWLEDGE

COMMUNITY WILDLIFE HABITATS

The National Wildlife Federation has certified entire communities as Community Wildlife Habitats. Communities in California, Washington, Virginia, Indiana, and Georgia have been certified. Many others around the country are working toward Community Wildlife Habitat certification.

▼ Discuss your plans with neighbors. Gardens that provide wildlife habitat look much different from those with conventional landscaping.

As you develop your Backyard Wildlife Habitat plan, talk to your neighbors about your ideas, so they will understand the importance of restoring habitat and the landscape you are trying to create. Check with your local municipal authorities and homeowners' association regarding lawn care and weed control. In some areas, it may not be legal to establish a meadow or to create brush piles. Sometimes these regulations are based on safety principles like fire prevention, but often they are based on nothing more than conventional suburban landscaping aesthetics. For information on developing habitat friendly weed ordinances, visit Wild Ones Natural Landscapers at www.for-wild.org.

Since a naturalistic landscape can look very different from a conventional one, inform your neighbors of your plans. Try to educate them on the importance of restoring habitat and share with them the wonders of a sustainable, wildlife-friendly landscape whenever possible. Select native plant species that have ornamental value as well as habitat value. Add definition to your more wild-looking plantings with a mulched border or a mown strip. Offer to share seeds or divisions of your native habitat-providing plants with neighbors. Hold an open house or neighborhood block party in your habitat to show neighbors the beauty of the habitat garden and to allow them to connect with wildlife. Join a garden club, or start one on your own, to teach others about the needs of wildlife and how gardens can be more than just pretty landscaping.

BEYOND YOUR BACKYARD

By creating a wildlife-friendly garden or landscape and certifying it with the National Wildlife Federation as a Backyard Wildlife Habitat site, you've demonstrated your commitment to making a difference for wildlife and the planet. Through the process, you've probably learned an incredible amount about how the actions you take in your own backyard have an impact on the ecological health of your community. As your time, energy, and confidence permit, take on new challenges and help spread the Backyard Wildlife Habitat message. Go beyond your backyard to help develop wildlife habitats for public use.

Habitats at Schools Facilities. A habitat area at your local school provides excellent educational opportunities and will be a source of community pride.

Workplace Habitats. Many businesses have large properties that could be managed as productive habitat areas. By allowing these areas to "go natural," a significant amount of habitat can be restored for use by resident and migratory wildlife.

Neighborhood Open Space. Homeowners' associations often oversee common grounds and other neighborhood open spaces that offer great opportunities for wildlife gardening and habitat restoration. Check with your local parks department about helping to make your town's park system an important resource for wildlife as well as people.

Faith Habitats. The message of stewardship of the Earth is a key component of many religious traditions. What better way of expressing that sentiment than by giving some space back to our fellow creatures?

Habitats as Places of Solace. The opportunity to be surrounded by beautiful natural landscapes and to view wildlife can be therapeutic for all people. New Yorkers and others around the world flocked to community gardens in the wake of the September 11, 2001, terrorist attacks as places of solace and quiet where they could deal with their shock and grief. The staff and residents of hospitals, pediatric care units, long-term care facilities, and assisted living complexes can benefit from connecting with nature through a wildlife habitat.

▲ Spread the word beyond your backyard. Above volunteers work to establish habitat in an open public space.

▼ By establishing a Backyard Wildlife Habitat garden you've made a commitment to local wildlife and the health of the planet as well.

119

REQUIREMENTS FOR CERTIFICATION

You may be closer to providing natural habitat for wildlife than you think. Use this checklist to assess your yard to determine which elements of habitat you are already providing for wildlife. Then use this information as a guide in your planning and planting to fill in those elements that you are currently missing.

For more information on habitat certification, visit National Wildlife Federation's Web site www.nwf.org/certify or call 800-822-9919.

Plant Foods:
☐ Seeds   ☐ Nuts
☐ Berries   ☐ Fruits
☐ Nectar   ☐ Sap
☐ Foliage/Twigs   ☐ Pollen

Feeder Types:
☐ Tube   ☐ Platform
☐ Suet   ☐ Hummingbird
☐ Squirrel   ☐ Butterfly

WATER: Wildlife need a clean water source for drinking and bathing. How do you provide water for wildlife?
☐ Birdbath   ☐ Water Garden/Pond
☐ Lakefront   ☐ Riverfront
☐ Stream   ☐ Puddling Area
☐ Seasonal Pond   ☐ Wetland
☐ Coastal   ☐ Spring

COVER: Wildlife need places to find shelter from the weather and from predators. How do you provide cover for wildlife?
☐ Wooded Area   ☐ Dense Shrubs/Thicket
☐ Bramble Patch   ☐ Evergreens
☐ Ground Cover   ☐ Brush Pile
☐ Log Pile   ☐ Rock Pile/Wall
☐ Caves   ☐ Meadow/Prairie
☐ Roosting Box   ☐ Burrows
☐ Water Garden/Pond

PLACES TO RAISE YOUNG: In order to provide complete habitat, you must provide places for wildlife to engage in courtship behavior and to mate, and then to bear and raise their young. How do you provide places to raise young for wildlife?
☐ Mature Trees   ☐ Dead Trees/Snags
☐ Meadow/Prairie   ☐ Dense Shrubs/Thicket
☐ Nesting Box   ☐ Water Garden/Pond
☐ Wetland   ☐ Burrows
☐ Caves   ☐ Host Plants for Caterpillars

PLANT LIST: Plant communities form the foundation of habitat for all wildlife. Plants that are native to your region are best. Please check the plant types that grow in your habitat. You may also list as many species as you can identify in the space provided.
☐ Evergreen trees   ☐ Deciduous trees
☐ Evergreen shrubs   ☐ Deciduous shrubs
☐ Cacti/succulents   ☐ Aquatic plants
☐ Wildflowers   ☐ Ferns   ☐ Other
☐ Vines   ☐ Grasses and grass-like plants

Plant Species: _____

SUSTAINABLE GARDENING PRACTICES: How you manage your garden or landscape can have an effect on the health of the soil, air, water and habitat for native wildlife—as well as the human community. What sustainable gardening techniques do you employ to help conserve resources?

Water Conservation:

- ☐ Vegetative Buffer Zone Around Water Feature
- ☐ Rain Garden
- ☐ Capture Rain Water from Roof
- ☐ Xeriscape
- ☐ Drip or Soaker Hose for Irrigation
- ☐ Reducing Lawn Areas
- ☐ Reducing Erosion
- ☐ Mulching
- ☐ Eliminating Chemical Pesticides
- ☐ Eliminating Chemical Fertilizers

Soil Conservation:

- ☐ Mulching ☐ Composting
- ☐ Reducing Erosion
- ☐ Eliminating Chemical Pesticides
- ☐ Eliminating Chemical Fertilizers

Controlling Exotic Species:

- ☐ Monitor Nesting Boxes
- ☐ Keeping Your Cat Indoors
- ☐ Removing Invasive Plants
- ☐ Restoring Native Plants
- ☐ Reducing Lawn Areas

Organic Practices:

- ☐ Eliminating Chemical Pesticides
- ☐ Eliminating Chemical Fertilizers
- ☐ Encouraging Pest Predators
- ☐ Composting

NATIONAL WILDLIFE FEDERATION

Protecting wildlife through education and action since 1936, the National Wildlife Federation® (NWF) is America's largest conservation organization. NWF works with a nationwide network of state affiliate organizations, scientists, grassroots activists, volunteers, educators, and wildlife enthusiasts, uniting individuals from diverse backgrounds to focus on three goals that will have the biggest impact on the future of America's wildlife.

CONNECT PEOPLE WITH NATURE

NWF is committed to volunteer and education programs that connect people to nature and wildlife. NWF magazines, including Ranger Rick®, Your Big Backyard®, Wild Animal Baby®, and National Wildlife®, educate adults and children about nature and conservation. NWF's Certified Wildlife Habitat™ program teaches individuals, schools, and communities how to create wildlife supporting habitat. Green Hour™ (www.greenhour.org) encourages parents to help their kids explore the outdoors for an hour each day.

PROTECT AND RESTORE WILDLIFE

Loss of habitat is a major threat to the future of America's wildlife. NWF works tirelessly to gain permanent protection for critical habitat areas that are essential to the recovery of endangered species. NWF also works to protect lands like the pristine Arctic National Wildlife Refuge, wild areas of the western U.S., and the forests of the Northeast. NWF focuses on restoring major waters and wetlands, including the Great Lakes, the Snake River, the Florida Everglades, and Puget Sound. NWF is committed to upholding the full protection of the Endangered Species Act, which has been the primary tool for conserving endangered and threatened species and their habitats.

CONFRONT GLOBAL WARMING

Human activities, such as burning of fossil fuels, have caused global warming. As average global temperatures increase, changing weather patterns are affecting wildlife. It is the single biggest ecosystem emergency we face today. Scientists predict that unless we act one-third of wildlife species in some regions could be headed for extinction within the next 50 years. NWF is taking action now to help halt global warming. Visit www.nwf.org/globalwarming for more information.

NWF relies on Americans from all walks of life, of all political and religious beliefs, of all ages to advance our mission: protecting wildlife for our children's future. Visit www.nwf.org or call 800-822-9919 to join today!

Glossary

Alien Species see Exotic Species

Bacillus thuringiensis (Bt) A type of soil bacteria used as an insecticide. Different strains of Bt are toxic only to specific groups of insect pests. Bt does not harm other forms of wildlife or humans.

Balled-and-burlapped A method of selling large woody plants where the root and soil ball is wrapped in burlap.

Bare-root A method of selling woody and herbaceous plants where the soil or other planting medium has been washed away from the rootball.

Beneficial insect These are predatory insects that keep the populations of aphids, certain caterpillars, and other plant-eating garden pests in check.

Bog A type of wetland formed when dead vegetation accumulates in a body of water faster than it can decompose, forming peat.

Brush pile A pile of woody debris that is carefully constructed to provide cover and places to raise young for wildlife.

Bunch grass Grasses that form clumps and do not spread by vegetative runners as turf grass does. Most North American native grasses are bunch grasses.

Carnivore A type of consumer that obtains nutrients by primarily eating the flesh of other consumers.

Cavity nester A species that typically builds nests and bears its young in tree holes or other natural cavities.

Chloramine A chemical added to some municipal water sources that kills microorganisms. It is toxic to fish, amphibians, and aquatic invertebrates.

Communities The naturally balanced groupings of plants, wildlife, and other organisms in a self-supporting ecosystem.

Consumer Species that obtain nutrients by eating plants or other wildlife species. See Food Chain.

Controlled burn A fire deliberately set and controlled to replicate the natural, periodic fires to which prairie and some forest plant communities are naturally adapted.

Conventional garden/landscape practice Gardening or landscaping practices that do not take the needs of wildlife into account. Conventional gardens and landscapes are made up primarily of lawn and ornamental plants.

Cultivar A specially bred or cloned variety of a plant.

Deciduous A plant that seasonally loses all of its foliage and goes dormant.

Decomposer An organism that obtains nutrients from the dead parts of plants or animals and returns nutrients to the soil. See Food Chain.

Diatomaceous earth A non-toxic substance made up of tiny, sharp silica particles used to kill soft-bodied insect pests.

Ecology The branch of biology that studies the interactions among living organisms, as well as the interactions among living organisms and the surrounding environment.

Ecosystem Balanced, self-sustaining interactive communities of plants and wildlife.

Ectotherm A species that relies on environmental conditions to regulate body temperature rather than producing heat internally.

Edge effect The increase in the number of species that occurs where two ecosystems meet.

Emergent plant A plant species that naturally grows in wet soils and shallow standing water.

Evergreen A plant species that does not lose the majority of its foliage seasonally.

Exotic species A species introduced to a new ecosystem by human activity.

Fallow field An agricultural field that is left unseeded and allowed to grow wild for a season or several seasons as a means of naturally restoring nutrients to the soil. Fallow fields are also used by wildlife.

Feral animal Domestic animal that is not cared for by humans. Feral animals prey on and compete with native species for resources.

Fledgling A young bird that has developed its flight feathers and left the nest but cannot fly. Fledglings spend several days on the ground or in low bushes and are fed by their parents.

Food chain The path of nutrients through the living components of an ecosystem. The food chain is made up of producers, consumers, and decomposers.

Forb An herbaceous plant that is not a grass.

Fungicide A pesticide designed to kill fungus.

Generalist species A species that can adapt to a variety of environmental conditions and can often live in close proximity to humans.

Girdling The process of killing woody vegetation by cutting through the outer bark around the entire base of the trunk and severing the plant's vascular system.

Gray water Water that is first used to wash clothing or dishes, and then it is used to water inedible landscape plants.

Green manure A crop turned into the soil rather than harvested. This is an organic method of returning nutrients such as nitrogen to the soil.

Habitat The collection of elements in an ecosystem that wildlife need to survive. The elements of habitat needed by all wildlife species are food, water, cover, and places to raise young.

Herbaceous plant A plant that has fleshy stems that die back to the ground during the dormant season.

Herbicide A pesticide designed to kill plants.

Herbivore A type of consumer that primarily obtains nutrients by eating plants.

Herptile This is a collective term for reptiles and amphibians.

Host plant A plant that serves as a food source for butterfly and moth caterpillars.

Hybrid A type of plant created by crossing two varieties of plants.

Insecticide A pesticide designed to kill insects and other invertebrates.

Insectivore A type of carnivore that feeds primarily on insects.

Integrated pest management (IPM) An approach to pest control that strives to manage pests at acceptable levels rather than eliminating them completely. It begins with techniques that are least harmful to the environment, such as planting resistant varieties, using biological controls, and applying less toxic sprays, and only resorts to traditional synthetic pesticides when the other methods have failed.

Invasive species An exotic species that has been introduced by humans into a new ecosystem and that spreads rampantly, outcompeting and eliminating the species native to that ecosystem.

Marsh A treeless wetland area.

Meadow Transitional native grassland community that occurs in areas with enough rainfall to support the growth of trees.

Microclimate The climate of a small specific place within a larger area as contrasted with the climate of the entire area.

Monoculture An area where only one plant species grows. Commonly used in agricultural terms, but it also refers to areas infested by invasive exotic plants.

Mixed grass prairie Native grassland community that includes wildflowers and grasses that grow between 2 and 5 feet tall.

Mosquito dunk A product that contains a strain of the bacteria Bacillus thuringiensis that will kill mosquito larvae without effecting most other wildlife or humans.

Mulch Any material used to cover bare soil to prevent erosion, retain moisture, and protect plant roots. Materials used for mulch include chipped or shredded bark, dead leaves, grass clippings, pine needles, straw, aged sawdust, shredded newspaper, gravel, and plastic.

Native species A species that evolved in an ecosystem over the course of thousands or millions of years and is part of that ecosystem's balanced community.

Naturalized species An exotic species that has established itself in the wild. Some naturalized species are invasive, while others are kept in check by the plants, animals, and other organisms native to the ecosystem.

Nestling A baby bird that has not developed its flight feathers and has not left the nest.

Nonnative species see Exotic Species

Omnivore A type of consumer that obtains nutrients by eating a mix of plant material and the flesh of other wildlife species.

Organic Pest control and fertilization practices that are not chemically based.

Pesticide A substance used to eradicate a plant, animal, or other organism deemed to be a pest to humans.

Pioneer species Plant species that colonize disturbed areas and can thrive in poor soil conditions. Pioneer species improve soil conditions and allow other more particular plants to colonize.

Plug A young herbaceous or woody plant grown in a small container and sold with a small rootball.

Pollination The process of moving pollen grains from the male parts of a flower to the female parts, resulting in fertilization and subsequent development of fruit and fertile seeds.

Pollinator A diverse group of wildlife that includes bees, butterflies, moths, flies, beetles, and other insects, as well as hummingbirds, bats, and other small mammals that are responsible for moving pollen and fertilizing plants.

Proboscis The straw-shaped mouth parts of butterflies and moths.

Producer Plants that use sunlight, water, and soil nutrients to create food for themselves in the form of carbohydrates. Producers are consumed by consumers. See Food Chain.

Rain barrel A barrel attached to a drainage downspout that collects and stores rainwater to be used in the landscape.

Root zone The area in which the roots of a tree or other plant grow.

Savannah Grassland with scattered pockets of trees and shrubs.

Scavenger An organism that feeds primarily on carcasses of other animals that it has not killed itself.

Shortgrass prairie A native grassland community composed of wildflowers and grasses that grow less than 2 feet tall.

Snag A standing dead tree.

Specialist species A species that requires a unique set of conditions and environment in order to survive.

Succession The natural changes in plant communities that occur after a disturbance.

Suet Rendered animal fat that can be used as a high-energy food source for birds in winter.

Swamp A wetland that supports trees.

Tallgrass prairie Native grassland community composed of wildflowers and grasses that grow 5 feet or taller.

Turf grass Grass species that spread sideways by vegetative runners as well as by seed. Lawns are typically composed of turf grasses of European and Asian species.

Variety A specific member of a species.

Vermicomposting Process of composting where worms are used to consume waste materials and produce nutrient-rich castings.

Vernal pool A small temporary pond that fills and dries up seasonally. These pools do not support fish, making them excellent breeding places for amphibians.

Water garden A relatively small, human-made pond or other container that holds water and plants.

Weed A subjective term referring to any plant that is considered undesirable in a given location.

Weed ordinance A local law specifying landscape restrictions, such as the maximum allowable height of herbaceous vegetation or the presence of dead standing trees or brush piles.

Whip A branch cutting of a woody plant that can be planted directly into the ground where it develops a root system and forms a new plant.

Wildflower A generic term for flowering herbaceous plants that includes both native plants as well as naturalized and invasive ones.

Woody debris Fallen dead trees or parts of trees.

Woody plant Refers to plants that have rigid stems covered in bark that do not die back to the ground seasonally.

Index

Index

Index

PHOTO CREDITS

All photos copyright of respective photographers, pages 1, 2, and 6: Daybreak Imagery **page 7:** *top* Connie Toops; *bottom* Daybreak Imagery **pages 8–12:** *all* Daybreak Imagery **page 13:** *top* Connie Toops **page 14:** Daybreak Imagery **page 15:** *top* Connie Toops; *center* Daybreak Imagery **pages 16–18:** *all* Connie Toops **page 19:** Daybreak Imagery **pages 20–22:** Connie Toops **pages 23–24:** Daybreak Imagery **page 25:** *top* George Harrison; *center* Connie Toops; *bottom* Daybreak Imagery **page 26:** Daybreak Imagery **page 27:** courtesy of Wild Birds Unlimited **page 28:** *top* George Harrison; *bottom* Daybreak Imagery **page 29:** *top left & right* Connie Toops; *center* George Harrison; *bottom* Connie Toops **page 30:** Daybreak Imagery **page 31:** *top* courtesy of Wild Birds Unlimited; *center* George Harrison; *bottom* courtesy of Wild Birds Unlimited **page 32:** *top* courtesy of Wild Birds Unlimited; *bottom* George Harrison **pages 33–34:** *all* Daybreak Imagery **page 35:** *top* Daybreak Imagery; *bottom* courtesy of Wild Birds Unlimited **pages 36–41:** Amy Leinback **page 42:** *both* Connie Toops **page 43:** Daybreak Imagery **page 44:** Connie Toops **page 45:** *top* George Harrison; *bottom* Daybreak Imagery **pages 46–47:** Daybreak Imagery **page 48:** *top* Daybreak Imagery; *center* Connie Toops; *bottom* Daybreak Imagery **page 49:** Connie Toops **page 50:** *top* Daybreak Imagery; *bottom* Connie Toops **page 51:** *top* George Harrison; *bottom* Jerry Pavia **page 52:** *left* Jerry Pavia; *right* Connie Toops **page 53:** *top* Gerry Bishop; *center* Connie Toops; *bottom* Daybreak Imagery **page 56:** Jerry Pavia **page 57:** *top* Daybreak Imagery; *bottom* Connie Toops **page 58:** *top* Pat Toops; *bottom* Gerry Bishop **page 60:** *both* George Harrison **pages 61–62:** Jerry Pavia **page 63:** George Harrison **page 64:** Jerry Pavia **page 65:** Connie Toops **page 66:** *top* Daybreak Imagery; *bottom* Jerry Pavia **page 67:** Daybreak Imagery **page 68:** *top* Daybreak Imagery; *bottom* Jerry Pavia **page 69:** Connie Toops **page 70:** Gerry Bishop **page 71:** Jerry Pavia **page 72:** George Harrison **page 73:** *both* Connie Toops **page 74:** *top* Daybreak Imagery; *bottom* Connie Toops **page 75:** Jerry Pavia **page 76:** *both* Daybreak Imagery **page 77:** *top* George Harrison; *bottom* Jerry Pavia **page 78:** *top* Jerry Pavia; *bottom left* Connie Toops; *bottom right* Daybreak Imagery **page 80:** Daybreak Imagery **page 81:** Gerry Bishop **page 82:** George Harrison **page 83:** *both* Daybreak Imagery **page 84:** *top & bottom left* George Harrison; *bottom right* Daybreak Imagery **page 86:** Daybreak Imagery **page 87:** *all* Daybreak Imagery; **page 88:** *both* Amy Leinbach **page 89:** *bottom left & top right* Connie Toops; *bottom right* Daybreak Imagery **page 90:** *top & bottom right* Daybreak Imagery; *bottom left* Connie Toops **page 92:** Daybreak Imagery **pages 93–95:** *all* Connie Toops **pages 96–97:** Daybreak Imagery **pages 98–99:** *left* Gerry Bishop; *center and right* Connie Toops **page 100:** George Harrison **page 102–106:** *all* Connie Toops **page 109:** *top & center* Daybreak Imagery; *bottom* Jerry Pavia **page 112:** *both* Connie Toops **page 113:** Jerry Pavia **pages 114–115:** Connie Toops **page 116:** Daybreak Imagery **page 117:** Gerry Bishop **page 118:** Connie Toops **page 119:** *top* Connie Toops; *bottom* Daybreak Imagery